D0856883

TALES
from
PINEHURST
STORIES FROM THE
MECCA OF AMERICAN GOLF

ROBERT HARTMAN

Sports Publishing L.L.C.
www.sportspublishingllc.com

Photos provided by The Tufts Archives, unless otherwise noted.

Director of production: Susan M. Moyer
Project managers: Tracy Gaudreau and Greg Hickman
Developmental editors: Gabe Rosen, Scott Rauguth and Mark E. Zulauf
Photo editor: Erin Linden-Levy
Copy editor: Holly Birch
Dust jacket design: Joseph Brumleve

ISBN: 1-58261-551-9

Printed in the United States.

Sports Publishing L.L.C.
www.sportspublishingllc.com

To Weston Moore, Emma Catherine,
and Ryan Bradford

Contents

Foreword vi

Acknowledgments xiv

Introduction xviii

Chapter 1 A Timeless Symbol 1

Chapter 2 The North and South Championship 19

Chapter 3 The U.S. Open 37

Chapter 4 Donald Ross 83

Chapter 5 Two Diverging Paths 101

Chapter 6 Changing Places 113

Chapter 7 More Than Just a Course 119

Chapter 8 The Old and the Young............................. 133

Chapter 9 The Outward Nine 141
The Inward Nine 148

Chapter 10 Pinehurst: The Village 155

Chapter 11 The Caddies 171

Chapter 12 The LPGA at Pinehurst 175

Chapter 13 The U.S. Amateur 179

Chapter 14 The PGA Tour 195

Epilogue 199

Foreword

I first came to Pinehurst in 1943. I was home from the war and I came over from Fort Bragg, NC, where I was spending time on the artillery range. It was a Sunday when the range was closed. In the summer of 1943, Pinehurst was not at its best, it was enduring the warm summer heat. But, as I look back, Fort Bragg was even warmer.

And I didn't play golf then, I just visited. But Pinehurst was well known to me as a young golfer since I had played in my first U.S. Amateur in 1938. So I knew some of the history. I was just intrigued to see the place. As a golf enthusiast, the aura around Pinehurst and the design of the golf courses and the community is like no other. Then, the North and South Amateur became an annual ritual, actually a family habit. After I married in 1954, my wife and I didn't go many places, but she made an exception with Pinehurst. She loved going down there.

I'm thinking of Pinehurst, in April, when the North and South was held. The azaleas and dogwoods were in bloom, and it was in its glory.

And Pinehurst No. 2 is my favorite course anywhere. And that's despite the lack of any water hazard. Sometimes other courses reach too far, it seems to me, to create something that is different. But Pinehurst has values, it has shot values, it has atmosphere and the atmosphere it has is basically seaside links-style golf. The anomaly of course, is that you don't have the seaside, which historically you once had, because obviously that is where the sand came from. But what Pinehurst has is closest to seaside links golf in America, and I am sure that is one of the reasons Donald Ross reacted favorably to the engagement by the Tufts family when he was brought down there in 1901 to become the resident professional adviser.

I have been a proponent of the Donald Ross designs and even more so of his personal philosophy. I just played Essex Country Club in Windsor, Ontario (1929). You need not be told that it was a Donald Ross design. It had flawless Donald Ross features. The greens were fair, with undulations, but not severely so. Bunkers are placed strategically, but are not pressing closely in on greens. Donald Ross always gave you a route to roll the ball onto the green. And he wasn't building golf courses for real estate development. Ross was building golf courses for golfers. The other thing that I found interesting was that they told me the Essex course was flat land, but in fact, the fairways were more like what the players face in the British Open at Royal St. Georges in Sandwich, England. And that was a feature brought over here by Ross from his days in Dornoch, Scotland. I am satisfied that Donald Ross created those dipsey doodles all over the fairways. Not severe ones. He didn't design golf courses for golf carts; he designed golf courses for their playability.

As far as his philosophy goes, I am a friend with Jim Simpson, who is the former Dean of the Dornoch Cathedral in Scotland. And he was moderator of the Church of Scotland, which is the original Presbyterian Church. He spoke at Pinehurst in 1989 at the Village Chapel when he was on a preaching mission. He told me of this sermon in which he quoted a bit of the Donald Ross philosophy. He said, "Americans seem to think that a well-hit drive should land and stay in the fairway and provide a fair lie and a flat stance to allow an approach to a receptive green with a makeable putt. By the same token: if you live a good life, it will all turn out well. But we Scots know better. We know that bad breaks and bad bounces do occur. You don't always get what you deserve in golf or in life. However, we cling to the thought that from a bad spot, we might make a great recovery, which of course, is our hope for redemption."

I often think of this very philosophy when I meet a Ross course at Essex or Pinehurst No. 2. He puts in bounces where even though you land in the fairway, it can end up anywhere. And that's golf.

To understand Pinehurst and amateur golf, let's go back in history. Originally, some of the great players of the early game were not amateurs, but professionals. Professionals in those days didn't make much money; I am talking about the Scottish days, where golf had its beginnings. And the game evolved early to people playing matches that involved some money. There were all kinds of challenge matches between leagues with Scottish players and later involving people from England. This was important to the evolution of the competitive game of golf as we know it. This group, which was made up of several clubs, eventually became known as the governing body of the Open Championship in 1860, in Prestwick.

When Tom Morris Jr., won the Open Belt (the Challenge Belt—similar to an archery or jousting trophy) for the third time, the Belt disappeared. There was no Open Championship because of it. But the leading local clubs got together and the British Open evolved from a Scottish event to a British event. And later at the request of the leading clubs in Britain, the Royal and Ancient Golf Club agreed to have its rules of golf committee serve as such for the entire game. It took the R&A 11 years from the time the initial request was made to seize it. But it took only five months from the time the R&A recommended it themselves before it was enacted by their spring and fall meeting (April/September). By the end of that year in 1892, the R&A had become the governing body. But the clubs were the ones who to this day are the hosts for the Open Championship. This is important, because the USGA was the governing body from 1897, when the rules of golf of the governing body became the rules of golf for the game. This happened in May of 1897. Meanwhile, two and a half years earlier in December of 1894, the USGA was formed as the governing body of America (Curiously, the same year Pinehurst was formed). The point is that the USGA is the senior governing body to the R&A.

This is the overall context. After 30 years of people playing for money, the game was then formerly developed and grew, thanks to the Victorian cycle of new golf clubs and the Caledonian Age of sporting people. The game of golf became established as the proper thing for gentlemen to do.

The U.S. Amateur became the main event, played first at the Newport Club in Rhode Island. The Open Championship was scheduled the next day as an add on. And as the Victorian age flourished, golf became part of it.

It's also true that we were fortunate that some of the great players of the amateur game were still name players in the professional game in Britain and this country. Bob Jones was the most famous of these, but he was not the first.

Walter Travis, for example, won three U.S. Amateurs in four years, and he also won the British Amateur in 1904. He created quite a furor because he used the center-shafted putter, the Schenectady putter, which was finally banned in 1909. The center-shafted putter and the stymie were at the center of the negotiations in 1951 when the R&A and the USGA got together to discuss the merging of the rules of golf. They were fighting mad that a non-Brit won the British Amateur Championship.

The game was growing with both great amateur players and great professional players in Britain and America. From the Jones era through 1930, in roughly half of the Open Championships in this country, an amateur either won or was runner-up. You might say that the amateur was the main driver of the competitive game.

I gave a talk at the Centennial of the U.S. Amateur in 1995 (won by Tiger Woods) at the Newport Club in Rhode Island. I asked, "What is the amateur spirit?" It is something Dick Tufts thought and felt very strongly about. Golf and sportsmanship include two basic elements, courtesy and integrity. And of course, rules of etiquette are more about attitude than they are behavioral. And the Bob Jones award for sportsmanship, which is the USGA's highest honor, is given annually to amateurs and professionals in honor of the tradition of the amateur spirit. Fortunately we haven't lost all that.

Most of the ink in this country goes to the PGA Tour, and rightly deserved, as it is a great show and great entertainment. But the rules of golf are based on the self-policing requirements of the game. In 1999, at the Ryder Cup at the Country Club in Boston, there was some commentary in the press that American golf was becoming like American football, basketball, baseball and hockey, with some thinking crowd heckling was a good idea. But golf is a different game. It is an individual game built on respect between competitors. The foundation is integrity and courtesy—courtesy among the players, courtesy extended from the crowds to the players and vice-versa. This is basic to the amateur game and actually the amateur spirit—regardless of whether it's applied to amateurs or professionals.

The legacy of amateur golf is vital, and no matter how successful we are on the PGA Tour, we should not lose sight of where we came from.

I saw Pinehurst as a place that not only offered a special golfing experience, but as one that I thoroughly enjoyed as a person. You get away from the world and go to Pinehurst and it's a place to escape in order to find one's self. I think golf brings out the best in people; if it doesn't, people are playing the wrong sport. And it should be that way whether they play well or not. I think Pinehurst, under the Tufts regime and now with Club Corp, is trying to not lose sight of the Tufts traditions. The management recognizes that this is a special place to be, regardless of the competition. And I have found after Pinehurst hosting the U.S. Amateurs, the U.S. Senior Open, the U.S. Women's Open, the World Amateur Team Championship and the U.S. Open, that people are seeing the best golf, the best of the golf course, the best atmosphere around them, and maybe more importantly, the best of themselves. I can't imagine a more beneficial experience than to spend a few days at Pinehurst. It is such a fulfilling experience.

I don't want to be too whimsical, but I can appreciate going out on the Village Green behind the pines near the Community Chapel and finding a place to sit and read.

People might think I'm strange, but I want to explain the side of golf that to me is somewhat *mystical*. This story will help explain why I feel this way. In 1950, (the first of my two North and South titles), I played Wynsol K. Spencer (Newport News VA/James River), who beat Frank Stranahan in the semifinals. And on the 35th hole, I had about a four and a half foot putt. We had a great crowd, but at this moment, the course was deadly silent. Before I putted to win the hole, the chimes at the Community Chapel tolled the hour of six. I stepped back and we all had a good laugh over it, because it was just as I was about to address the putt. There was a surreal quality to the event as I eventually made the putt to win the hole. On the 36th we both made pars, and I won the event with a birdie on the 37th. I had things going my way, and I was in tune. In a way, it was destiny.

But the odd part about the events at Pinehurst, about 30 days later I was playing at St. Andrews in the sixth round of the British Amateur, and ironically I was on the very same green, the 17th, against my opponent Joe Carr. A strong, cold wind came off the North Sea. I was over the green after hitting a five iron in two, and I hit it hard into the bank, and it finally got up and I had to make the five-foot putt. I had to make the putt. The cold wind was coming up my calves, and the appearance of the cup was turning to fuzz, and so was the golf ball. And the course was sparse with spectators and very quiet. Just as I stood over another crucial putt, the town clock in St. Andrews tolled the hour of six. I had no doubt about it. The putt was going to roll in dead center. It did.

William C. Campbell

William C. Campbell is the Cal Ripken of amateur golf. He played in a record 37 U.S. Amateurs (including 33 straight (1941-1977*). He won the U.S. Amateur in 1964 at the age of 41 and served as the president of the USGA from 1982-83. He is the only person to have served as the USGA president and the captain of the R&A. He is also a two-time North and South Amateur Champion.
*the amateur was not played from 1942-45.

Acknowledgments

When I was contacted about writing a book about special golf venues in America, my publisher said: *Pebble Beach or Pinehurst?*

Thank God I chose Pinehurst. Thank you Cathy for your faith walk in getting the project finished. Thank you for your faith walk every day.

I first visited Pinehurst in 1976. The fog had barely lifted from the fairways and my mouth when I realized that Pinehurst No. 2 was abominable.

In 1987, I arrived to see a different Pinehurst. I saw a young man named Jason Widener beat some of the best junior players in the country on newly opened Pinehurst No. 7. When I walked into the Village during my visit I remember thinking that this kind of Village must be artificial. Nowhere in America can you have a town that is seamless. A town that flows from beginning to end with such a natural harmony that it appears, well, perfect.

In 1998, I traveled into town from my home in Virginia thinking, "How did such a great expanse of golf course find its way here—in the middle of nowhere?" I walked into the Tufts Archives and an energetic staff greeted me: Liz Dowling, Audrey Moriarty (her husband works for *Golf Digest* and I called him, Mike, five times), Fred Heanline, John Root and Hellie Reed. Thank you for adding the finishing touches to this project. And to the staff at Pinehurst,

Beth Kocher, Reg Jones, Paul Jett, Don Padgett, Ken Crow, Kelly McCall, Jeff Ferguson, Charlie McRae and every stranger I stopped along the way. To Caleb Miles and Mary Kim, wow, it wouldn't have happened without your assistance.

To Bill Campbell, the only person ever to serve as the president of the USGA and the captain of the R&A. To Harvie Ward, Waddy Stokes, Phil Mickleson, Billy Joe Patton, Carol Semple Thompson, Mary Mickleson, John Derr, Jack Nicklaus, Simon Hobday, Ray Floyd, Arnold Palmer, Hal Sutton, Rod Innes, the Barretts and the staff at the Pine Crest. Scott Pattera exists, I am just not sure if I will ever find him. A lot of the information for this manuscript was crafted in room 222. Since Ross once owned the Pine Crest, I felt the need to allow his karma to echo on my laptop. I heard more golf stories in the dining room at the Pine Crest than anywhere else in Pinehurst. Some of the stories will have to stay there.

Thank you to my parents for introducing me to this tiny place 30 years ago. My dad still sets the golf standard in the family. Eric Trethewey at Hollins University and Roland Lazenby deserve credit for being the sounding blocks to my ranting.

Thanks to Tim and Sally Gold, Alan Riley, the Villager and a special thanks to Bob Tufts. Thanks to Richard Tufts, Donald Ross and Payne Stewart.

And to Gabe Rosen, Tracy Gaudreau and Mark Zulauf who somehow got this project to the 18th hole.

And most importantly, thank you to Ryan, Emma and Weston. Is daddy writing about Pinehurst anymore?

Not until June of 2005.

Introduction

Pinehurst is about yesterday as much as it is about to-morrow. Pinehurst is about restoration more than it is about developing. Pinehurst does not have a progressive attitude as much as it stays ahead by staying behind. Somewhere in the history of American golf, the word Pinehurst is going to ignite the senses to the wail of bagpipe music, the smell of fresh pines and the click of the club head meeting the ball. Pinehurst is more persimmon than metal, but the words golf and Pinehurst will long be married in a conversation—probably of stories of time spent on the hallowed grounds.

But *time* at Pinehurst is another matter. It can be successfully argued that time ticks slower at Pinehurst. And days of the week are a melting pot, just like months of the year. No one person stirs the pot at Pinehurst; it simmers into a never-ending conversation about a missed putt or a perfect approach shot gone awry.

Long-time amateur and former USGA president Bill Campbell once said, "Pinehurst is more than good golf courses. It's a state of mind…and heart."

A little more than 100 years have passed since James W. Tufts, the master of design, parlayed his soda fountain fortune into an effort to cultivate 6,000 acres into a resort where guests could take advantage of the Carolina climate.

Before Tufts arrived, the soil and dense Pine were used to manufacture turpentine and tar. When he did arrive and began to build a resort, it became a little more difficult than managing a chain of drugstores and soda fountain machines. And it was clear he was going to need a name for what workers were calling *Tufts Town*. Hearing of a contest near his summer home off Martha's Vineyard, Tuft asked about some of the runners up's names. From these he chose *Pinehurst*. He compensated the contestant and ventured south.

The first five years involved moving dirt and hammering and building the resort, which began with the Holly Inn. After five years of growth and new ideas, the Tufts family built the main hotel, the Carolina.

And then it happened. Around the turn of the 20th century, some were complaining that guests were using sticks and knocking a small wooden ball around, and they were disturbing the cattle. The cows did not moo their displeasure, but Tufts soon got to the bottom of the game...golf. A little-known fact is that the European sport had been a sport of shepherds as they knocked the balls around to steer their flock. At the urging of guests, Tufts began the construction of a nine-hole course. And he then hired Donald Ross to steer the efforts of this new sport. The agreement between Tufts and Ross would last 48 years and could be argued to be the most pivotal partnership in fostering the game in America.

Soon after the playing field was established, they began holding golf tournaments, the first being the United North and South tournament in 1901. For the first few years, the women competed with the men. This was until the women established their own amateur event a few years later. This was the true beginning. The sport was planting its roots, which, like everything at Pinehurst, seemed to spread best by word of mouth. Then, in 1902, James Tufts died at his apartment at the Carolina hotel. He bequeathed the entire resort to his son, Leonard Tufts.

The early years were as much about construction of the land as they were about cultivating the game. Like anything, this took time. Between 1901 and 1999, Pinehurst did something right. Was it the 1948 North and South where underdog Harvie Ward from the campus of North Carolina ousted the notorious Frank Stranahan in the finals, 1-up? Was it in 1940, when a 27-year-old pro named Ben Hogan drove into Pinehurst with little money left to compete on the pro circuit, and naysayers said, "With that swing he will never make it"? All Hogan did was earn his first professional title at Pinehurst. Did Pinehurst earn stripes in 1985, when the elder statesman of golf, Jack Nicklaus, walked with his son, Jack Nicklaus II to victory in the North and South? The next year Nicklaus senior made history at Augusta.

No one individual or one event signaled the arrival of Pinehurst, because Pinehurst really had no place to go and no reason to change. Pinehurst became known as the birthplace of American golf. It took the 1936 PGA, the 1951 Ryder Cup, the 1962 U.S. Amateur, and then a lot of refinement between 1962 and 1996 for the golfing decision makers to admit that Pinehurst was not forgotten. What really happened was that between 1962 and the years of the bright polyester colors, visors and the explosion of technology (both turf grass and golf hardware), Pinehurst was concerned with paying the bills. They were really concerned with selling condos and not so concerned with selling tee times and Titleists.

What Pinehurst did right was lay a foundation. It was one shot at a time, one brick at a time and one moment at a time. The late Don Padgett used to say time and time again, "Anyone who is anyone in the world of golf, had their picture taken on the steps of the Pinehurst Country Club."

In retrospect, Donald Ross made an immediate impression on the resort by serving as course designer, head pro, greenskeeper and general expert. By the mid-1960s, courses were beginning to realize the game was changing at a rapid rate. The care of the golf course was becoming a science implemented by people with an alphabet soup of degrees and army-like staff. Ross's never-ending tweaking of the layout at Pinehurst did not end until his death in 1948.

But the advent of turf and his trademark wiregrass, his methods of using plows and plantings really made Pinehurst possible. If Tufts was credited with the vision, Ross was equally credited with implementing the vision, from wiregrass and pine needles to the science of agronomy. Greenskeepers became superintendents, and head professionals became directors of golf. The game was speeding at a pace and like always, Pinehurst was not in a hurry. In due time, Pinehurst received the nod in the early 1990s to host the Women's Open at Pine Needles in 1996 and the Men's Open in 1999. Was it a turning point, or serendipity? The USGA really cares about this haven in North Carolina. It cares about the heritage, the tee boxes, the rough, the mower

Richard S. Tufts (left) and Donald J. Ross (right).

height, the stimpmeter readings, and it cares about the pinnable green surfaces so much, that it will make a return trip for the National Open.

Ask anyone around Pinehurst about the importance of the No. 2 course in the national ranking of America's finest courses and you get different answers. "Oh, certainly if we drop out of the top 10, I think we would hear about it," said Paul Jett, course superintendent. Caleb Miles, the director of the Convention and Vistor's Bureau, echoes that sentiment. "We are most proud of our recognition as one of America's top golfing destinations."

One of the most awe-inspiring aspects of the town of Pinehurst is the village. In many historical accounts,

Frederick Law Olmsted was given credit for the mature landscaping and contour of the garden scape at Pinehurst. The story is told that James Tufts did visit Olmsted, the same designer who is credited with the Biltmore in Asheville, NC. There was a meeting of Tufts and Olmsted, but the tiny North Carolina community was not a high priority for the renowned Olmsted. He said the land was "uninteresting" and did not have "any real possibilities." He deflected the work to a landscape associate, Warren Manning. Manning should get most of the credit for designing the endearing beauty of Pinehurst. Manning successfully cultivated the plantings despite the difficult sandy nature of the soil. Olmsted was initially given a contract for $300, and it was Manning who got his hands in the dirt. He oversaw tree plantings, flower beds and the importation of a French plant called a nandina.

Manning and Leonard Tufts mapped out the village. The line drawing became an oil painting, and the oil painting became a grand lady with gentle curves. There are no right angles in the village of Pinehurst. The roads go in sweeping directions; the pine trees and vegetation all provide a canopy effect on the town. It is an organized chaos of architecture and simplicity. One passerby says, "If you go through the town of Pinehurst in a big hurry, you've missed the whole point." The village is like a tall glass of iced tea. It is a town rich with thought and rich with an energy that people care about the daily activities around them. In most resort towns, there is a disjointed connection with the business district and the resort areas. In Pinehurst the connection to both is seamless.

Along with its on- and off-course landscape, Pinehurst is entrenched in the purest form of the game. The word *amateur* has never been lost. Not losing the word amateur in the marketing landscape of the PGA Tour and the modern advent of the game is like skipping Godiva for a vanilla wafer.

Pat Corso, president of Pinehurst during the Club Corp. days says, "The only thing that has changed at Pinehurst since 1900 is the vintage of the automobiles."

The clock is ticking slower and slower...

Simple golf. At Pinehurst the design of the golf courses is at the heart of the resort's reputation.

One Resort—Throughout One Century
——— A Timeline ———

People shape events, events shape lives, and with these experiences we grow. Pinehurst has evolved since 1895 through people who have impacted the events at a tiny bastion of life known as Pinehurst. See how the following events impacted the memories at the one place in America where there is no ticking clock.

Horses with plows led excavation efforts on the first golf courses at Pinehurst.

1895 (February)

James Walker Tufts purchases 6,000 acres of land for an average of one dollar per acre from a family in nearby Aberdeen. The land was referred to as wasted timberland and several people said that Tufts, a soda-pop magnate, might have just made a major mistake.

1895 (June)

Tufts recognizes the need for some plantings. He calls his office in New York and is then referred to a landscape architectural firm directed by a man named Olmsted. Frederick Law Olmsted visits the proposed grounds of the village and returns with a description of the area as "uninteresting." He adds, "I'll send Manning back in the fall." Olmsted was credited for developing a certain park in New York, called Central Park. They eventually respond by planting 200,000 trees and shrubs. This provides Pinehurst with a pine scent year round.

1895 (June—December)

The Holly Inn, General Office Building, General Store, 20 cottages and a row of homes are built in unprecedented time. Tufts's field of dreams begins to take shape.

1895 (December 31)

The Holly Inn opens its doors for business. Twenty guests arrive to a luxury environment, which features telephones, steam heat, electricity and an orchestra. The Holly closes its doors in April because summer is around the corner. The first Pinehurst season runs from October through

Excavating was an entirely different process at the turn of the century. But through the process came a wonderous golf course layout.

April until 1920. Tufts recognizes that the best use of his resort is as a "winter retreat."

1897
Town Hall opens on Christmas day.

1898 (March)
Tufts tires of hearing from the local dairymen. Guests were scaring the cows by hitting white wooden balls into their pasture. Tufts gives in to the pressure. LeRoy Culver designs a rudimentary nine-hole golf course. H.J. Heinz visits Pinehurst this year.

──────── *1898 (September)* ────────

Leonard Tufts, son of the owner, suggests changes to the golf course, initiating a turf management campaign. They also add a fence, build the first clubhouse and name the first pro, John Dunn Tucker.

──────── *1900 (March)* ────────

British amateur Harry Vardon plays four exhibition rounds at Pinehurst, offering a glowing report. This officially seals Pinehurst's grip on the golf industry during its early infancy.

──────── *1900 (June)* ────────

Scotsman Donald Ross is hired as the second golf professional. He tinkers with the design of the golf course, adding some subtle touches. He teaches hundreds to play golf and improve their game as it continues to gain popularity in America. He is really appointed to become head pro, greenskeeper, club maker and anything else that deals with golf in the sleepy southern village.

──────── *1901 (January)* ────────

The Carolina Hotel opens on New Year's Day, a premier hotel with 250 rooms. George C. Dutton wins the first North and South Championship with a 169. This was the only North and South decided by stroke play; A shot of 180 yards, eight inches, wins the driving contest. The tournament went on annually without interruption and eventually became the oldest continuous golfing event. Donald Ross develops the first nine holes of the second golf course.

1902

Jack Jolly, a professional from St. Andrews, Scotland, and Donald Ross, the Pinehurst golf course architect, cause a stir when they played a round of golf entirely by moonlight. Play takes three hours, and the golfers do not lose a single golf ball. James Walker Tufts dies of a heart attack at the Carolina; his son Leonard inherits Pinehurst.

1903

Donald Ross wins the first North and South Open with a 147. The first North and South Women's Amateur is played. There are 17 entrants, and Mrs. Myra D. Paterson wins 1-up over Miss Florence Bradbury. Paterson wins the 16th hole (496 yards) with a 10 to her opponent's 11.

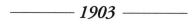

1904

Walter J. Travis, in winning the North and South Amateur, sets a course record of 69 that holds up until the event is moved to the No. 2 course. Alex Ross, Donald's brother, receives $100 for winning the first of five North and South Open titles.

1905

The Pinehurst Outlook, the area's seasonal newspaper, reports that J.D. Rockefeller returned home after a "visit to Pinehurst of many weeks."

1907

The 18 holes of Pinehurst No. 2 is opened. Ross proclaims his championship course to be "the fairest test of golf I have ever designed."

1909

James D. Standish, Jr., who later becomes president of the U.S. Golf Association, wins the North and South Amateur played over the No. 2 course.

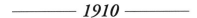

1910

Pinehurst No. 3 opens, also designed by Donald Ross. Ross decides that his design business needs more attention. He resigns as golf professional.

1911

Chick Evans Jr., defeats Walter J. Travis in the first round of the North and South Amateur. He goes on to win the title. This is Travis's first loss. He had played in 1904 and 1910 and won both times.

1916

Annie Oakley, the star of the "Buffalo Bill Wild West Show," comes to Pinehurst. She stays to give shooting exhibitions and lessons at the resort's Gun Club for many years to come.

1918

Irving S. Robeson wins the North and South Amateur, this completing the only father-son combination to win the title. His son, Filimore K., won in 1915.

1919

Eighteen holes of Pinehurst No. 4 opens, designed by Ross, who also continues to tinker and shape greens and holes on all the courses.

1920

A New Englander, Frances Ouimet, wins the North and South Amateur.

1921

The Pine Crest Inn is sold to Donald Ross and James McNabb.

1922

Leonard Tufts gets together with "well-to-do" residents to launch the Mid-Pines Country Club. Donald Ross designed the Mid-Pines golf course.

1926

George T. Dunlap Jr., becomes the first native of Pinehurst to win the North and South Amateur. He eventually wins the North and South seven times, the most titles anyone has ever won.

1928

The first nine holes of No. 5 are developed by Ross. They are abandoned seven years later.

1930

Leonard Tufts, in failing health, passes the Pinehurst reins to sons Richard, Albert and James.

1931

Amelia Earhart visits Pinehurst, landing her plane on the Pinehurst airstrip.

1933

George T. Dunlap Jr., defeats Johnny Johnson in 38 holes to win the longest North and South Amateur.

1934

Grass greens are experimented with on the No. 2 course.

1936

The PGA championship is held on the No. 2 course. Denny Shute beats one of the best long-ball hitters in the game, Jimmy Thomson. Shute's solid play earns him a 3 and 2 win.

1940

Ben Hogan shot 277 to win the North and South Open, scoring 280 to win his first professional title.

1944

Army chief of staff general George C. Marshall purchases his home in Pinehurst. It is rumored that Marshall's post-war European recovery was written while he stayed in Pinehurst.

1945

Lt. Cary Middlecoff wins the North and South Open as an amateur. Denny Shute finishes second and Ben Hogan third. Middlecoff, a dentist from Memphis, would turn professional in 1947. He would go on to win two U.S. Opens and a Masters.

1948

Frank Stranahan, who won the British, Canadian and Mexican Amateurs during the year, loses to Harvie Ward Jr. in the North and South Amateur finals, 1-up. Donald Ross dies. The Donald Ross Memorial Junior Tournament is inaugurated.

1951

The Ryder Cup Matches are held at Pinehurst No. 2. The United States team beats Great Britain nine and one half to two and one half. Richard Tufts is instrumental in the end of the North and South Open. Tommy Bolt wins the event and Tufts acknowledges, "The professionals had nothing to contribute to the development of a true golfing atmosphere at Pinehurst."

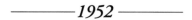
1952

Tufts sees fit to begin a new amateur event. The North and South Senior Men's Amateur is started.

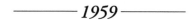
1959

Jack Nicklaus wins the North and South Amateur.

1960

Billy Joe Patton begins a petition to bring the U.S. Amateur to Pinehurst. Richard Tufts yields to the request. The USGA grants the tournament to Pinehurst No. 2 for 1964.

1961

Ellis Maples constructs Pinehurst No. 5.

1962

The U.S. Amateur is contested and won by Labron E. Harris when he sinks a putt on the final hole to beat Downing Gray, 1-up. Harris is five down after the first 18. He receives a call from his father, then the golf coach at Oklahoma State who said, "You can win—you've got it in you." But from 1959 to 1963, either Deane Beman or Jack Nicklaus won the U.S. Amateur.

1966

Jim Wiechers defeats Ron Cerrudo, 1-up in the finals of the Western Amateur, the first time the tournament visits Pinehurst.

1970

Pinehurst is sold to Diamondhead Corp.

1971

Pinehurst No. 2 serves as the site for the PGA Club Professionals Championship.

1973

The World Open is contested at Pinehurst No. 4.

1975

The Tufts Archives Wing is added to the Given Memorial Library in the village.

───────── *1979* ─────────

Pinehurst No. 6 is opened, designed by George and Tom Fazio, the first Pinehurst course built away from the core.

───────── *1984* ─────────

ClubCorp of America acquires Pinehurst.

───────── *1986* ─────────

Rees Jones designs Pinehurst No. 7. The Heritage Foundation holds its meeting at Pinehurst, drawing such dignitaries as Henry and Clare Booth Luce, Alexander Haig and Elizabeth Dole.

───────── *1989* ─────────

Vicki Goetze wins the U.S. Women's Amateur Championship.

───────── *1991* ─────────

Craig Stadler wins the Tour championship held on Pinehurst No. 2.

1992

Paul Azinger wins the Tour championship.

───────── *1994* ─────────

Simon Hobday claims victory at the U.S. Men's Senior Open.

───────── *1995* ─────────

Pinehurst celebrates its centennial.

1996

Pinehurst No. 8, the Centennial Course, opens. Designer Tom Fazio attends its inauguration. The Department of the Interior declares Pinehurst a National Historic Landmark.

1999

Pinehurst hosts the U.S. Open.

2000

Pinehurst No. 4, an entirely new course layout designed by Tom Fazio, opens to praise. Fazio calls it his "tribute to Pinehurst."

2002

The Pinehurst Spa opens adjacent to the Carolina Hotel.

2005

Pinehurst again serves as host to the U.S. Open.

1

A Timeless Symbol

Symbols, logos, phrases and other marketing icons conjure meaning in the American sports landscape. And in a place like Pinehurst, where time has tested them since the late 1800s, one ageless symbol has endured: The Putter Boy.

In the early days of Pinehurst, Frank Presbrey, a young advertising counselor, sought to create an image that would represent the spirit surrounding the burgeoning resort. Presbrey would grow into a well-known and sought-after advertising specialist, writing a book, *The History and Development of Advertising,* and developing images and campaigns.

For Pinehurst, Presbrey developed a young golfing character known in the early days as the "Golf Lad" or "Golf Boy." One of the early advertising pieces was a calendar that featured this same "Golf Calendar Lad" touting the resort as a golf destination and winter retreat. His image appeared on calendars, placemats and brochures. He always wore a floppy hat and carried a golf club. For Presbrey and Pinehurst, he represented a simple ideal. Here was a young man, seemingly happy, with a passion and a sense of purpose to play the game of golf. He was the common man who had a spirit that was evident in his expression and posture.

Today professional sports teams change colors and logos to sell more jerseys, hats and apparel. At Pinehurst, the Golfing Lad has never grown old. His symbol represents the early days, and it represents tomorrow. Reg Jones, member of the 2005 U.S. Open executive committee, says the new Open logo will again be the Putter Boy. "He has not gotten any older," said Jones. "For 2005, he has gotten a little more patriotic."

The logo has not gotten older, but it has evolved. In 1912, sculptress Lucy P.C. Richards sat down with bronze clay in her hands to mold a sundial. Her subject was Presbrey's menu advertising picture of the Golf Calendar Lad. Donald Ross heard Richards was hard at work and wanted to assist Richards with the design of the Putter Boy sundial. He showed up at her studio to show her the proper stance and the grip for the statue. There was a major problem with the sculpting. Richards wanted to make the shaft long to allow for proper right angles for accurate sundial readings. After all, this was a sundial, not a tip on how to properly hold the club and address the ball. Another purist problem with the Golfing Lad is the club. If you examine the original statue, it is clear that the Golfing Lad is holding not a putter, but a driver. The name grew from Golfing Lad, to the Sundial Boy until the 1970s, when the name Putter Boy was adopted. The Putter Boy logo has gone beyond the sun or moon when it comes to marketing. And while advertising executives claim that, "You always need a fresh look," the Putter Boy has evolved since the early days as a signature on shirts, hats, and every imaginable printed item in circulation. Tom Stewart, owner of a golf memorabilia shop in the village comments, "It has become a very visible logo, and you can pick up the sundial statue around town for the going price of around $1,000." Since landowners and winners of the North and South were the original holders of the Putter Boy statues, it has increased in value.

The bronze Putter Boys were once given away as real estate offerings. When people bought a piece of land during the 1970s, the Putter Boys were gifts at closing. In 1978, the Sundial made its way from the golf putting greens adjacent to the verandah, to the PGA World Golf Hall of Fame.

The Putter Boy has since been returned to the original home between the resort's two practice greens. When the first player tees up on June 16, 2005, the Putter Boy will be more than 100 years old.

Where to Begin

Many observers think that the first golf design expert at Pinehurst was Donald Ross. Wrong. In 1898, a disgruntled local dairy farmer approached James Tufts to discuss the golf ball-sized hail that was coming from a field. How could his cattle graze properly if wooden balls were bombing them? After researching the white wooden balls and tracing them back to the hickory shafted sticks being swatted by resort guests, Tufts came to a swift conclusion that they needed a place to hit these darn things. His initial frustration was discussed with an acquaintance, Dr. Leroy Culver, a physician in nearby Southern Pines. He asked Culver about what it would take to add the sport of golf to his resort offerings. Culver had two qualities that endeared him to Tufts: he loved the game, and he once played the game on a Scottish links course. He was hired. Culver was the original designer of golf at Pinehurst. He designed nine holes.

Mr. Ross

Maybe the best way to describe the advent of the game of golf in America is to travel to Scotland and England and observe the British Open. The shrill echo of Scottish bagpipe music is distinct, there is mist in the air, the wind and rain ignites the senses to golf's humble beginnings. Scotland—the place where unrestrained natural terrain gives way to the game's birthplace.

At the turn of the 20th century, the game of golf was just planting its roots in America. And at Pinehurst, Tufts was picking up the golf balls and trying to understand the significance of the game. This was not James Naismith and the peach basket. This was someone who casually observed and absorbed. He was one of many Americans who were simply trying to understand the game and its nuances.

As you continue to enjoy the softness of the bagpipes and the salty North Sea air while you take a refrain, remember that place in America in the 19th century that had little use. James Taylor was not yet singing "Carolina in My Mind." It was a raw desert. A plat of land in the North

Carolina sandhills region was functionally obsolete. The soil was too sandy, and the forest too dense with pine to even consider cultivating its limited value. Heck, it was not even very good to generate tar and turpentine. Yet James W. Tufts saw value in the rarefied air. He was not as interested in the soil as he was in the awesome climate. Meteorologist Tufts sought the mid-range temperatures and the afternoon shade from the tall pines. Tufts called it a *vacation for the senses*. And what better way to accommodate his passion for relaxation in the warm Carolina air, than build a resort?

The Pinehurst resort was born in 1895, a resort that allowed its guests to visit, pass the time and relax. It just so happens that some of the resting vacationers were being disturbed by the clank of wooden balls. It wasn't until a few friendly vacationers opined on what "Tufts really needed," that the grand designer even considered a game born in Scotland. With a nudge, Tufts decided his resort needed a golf course. In 1897, 60 acres were cleared, about a three-minute walk from the village of Pinehurst. The idea was to construct six and nine holes, just enough to catch the passing fancy of some of the guests who wanted to play that European game born in Scotland. Can you still hear the bagpipes?

About the same time Tufts was excavating pine in central North Carolina, a Harvard professor, Robert Wilson, became obsessed with golf. He traveled during his summers to Dornoch to become acquainted with the sport. One of his personal acquaintances was Donald Ross. At Wilson's urging, Ross, in 1899, spent his entire savings venturing to the new world. Wilson rewarded the young man by hiring him as the golf professional of Oakley Golf Club in Watertown, Massachusetts. Less than a year later, Tufts went north looking for golf professionals, and was introduced to Ross. An interview was set up at Tufts's house, down the road in Medford. Tufts found a young man with a passion for the game in Ross, who initially spent winters in Pinehurst and Watertown, and later Essex, during the summers. He saw the greater opportunity in Pinehurst and teamed with Frank Maples, the Pinehurst superintendent of courses. His technique for designing was born from his mentor, old Tom Morris. He learned the trades of club making, greenskeeping and design from Morris. Ross was taken by Pinehurst's rolling terrain, which reminded him of home. He was taken by the soil, and now he had the perfect blank canvas. He saw

Pinehurst in its early stages.

possibilities for carving more than just nine holes at
Pinehurst, courses that could allow a player to cover every
club in the bag and test the most challenging mind of the
game. Within a year of arriving at Pinehurst, Ross had completed his first nine holes, which later became the No. 2
course. In 1901, when the first nine holes were finished, the
course measured 2,275 yards. When the second nine were
finished in 1907, the total test was a mere 5,860 yards.

More than 100 years later, as amateurs and professionals analyze Pinehurst, they begin hitting the small greens
with long irons. They ramble and stumble about, getting
up and down from greenside hazards. Then they discuss the
overall test of the mind. Pinehurst has become the Wrigley
Field or Lambeau Field of golf. It has a historical bent that
few courses hold. It is the home of golf.

But Pinehurst is much more than that. Pinehurst has
become frozen in time as a small-town slice of Americana
where thousands of vacationers come to relax, just as Tufts
had planned in 1895. The village offers a non-commercial
district, the landscaping is in bloom full season and the architecture is decidedly southern. It just so happens that
Pinehurst is a throwback. As the technology of golf has grown
in gigabytes, Pinehurst has stood the test of time through
its refusal to compromise its individuality. It is truly an original—original and tough. In the 1999 U.S. Open, Payne
Stewart and Phil Mickelson showed up on the 72nd hole,
battling to beat even par. Even par was just how Ross would
have wanted it. From Azinger to Zoeller, they shake their
heads in disbelief and put it in a category that begs the elite.
Pebble Beach, Pine Valley, Oakmont, Oakland Hills

and…Pinehurst. It is not easy to identify one singular reason for its difficulty. The courses, through several modifications, were unmistakably demanding and yet very simple. Ross's course layout methods were unique. He first positioned the sandy greens and then contoured the hole back to the tee. His imagination was complex—he knew he wanted to provide a stern test to the ultimate manager of the game of golf, yet nothing was done with the terrain to render gimmicks. There was subtle positioning and a premium on preciseness. The smallish convex greens reminded him of his homeland. The bunkers were strategically placed and provided enough penalties to most players without being punishing.

Ross was fair, so in most cases he allows the player who often plays a low shot unimpeded entrance to the green. At Pinehurst, the flow of the golf courses has as much to do with the layout than, say, a sloping green or severe dogleg. His passion for the game is found in the simplistic way Ross delicately carved between the mature landscapes that nature allowed.

Golf's beginnings at Pinehurst were humble but assertive. Tufts and Ross knew they had something special from the start. They knew the basics they were establishing might be better for the time-tested player. The game was just developing a momentum that offered players at the time an alternative to the very early courses in the northeast. When the chill of winter came, the Pinehurst resort boasted a warm climate. But there was more. The game in Pinehurst was evocative of the Scottish-born courses. The difficulty lies in the players' ability to manage the ball off the tee, then to position the approach shot in a way that par or better is possible. Likewise, if St. Andrews is the home of golf, so too is Pinehurst the home of golf.

Ross never stopped tweaking the playing field. And the USGA never stops tweaking the playing field. The USGA credo may as well be "Faster (greens), taller (rough) and longer (playing yards)."

Ross created a masterpiece from scratch. He molded, sculpted, refined and pioneered the most subtle aspects of the playing field. USGA executive director David Fay said, "The United States may not have a St. Andrews, but Pinehurst is the closest thing to St. Andrews we have in terms of the feel for the history of the game, the passion of the game. The whole place just exudes golf."

Some things never change. Hear the bagpipes, smell the pines and hit the ball.

Field of Dreams

Magnolia Lane, the pounding surf on the rocks at Pebble Beach, the walk from the clubhouse to the first tee at Pinehurst. The steps begin from the historic clubhouse. Then, past the large putting greens, the bronze sundial of the Putter Boy and the statues of Donald Ross, Richard Tufts and Payne Stewart. This is all part of the soft-spike walk to the first tee at No. 2. Like the beginning of a classic novel, the experience of playing Pinehurst No. 2 begins to take hold when you are greeted at the starter's desk, where there is a monument with a message from Donald Ross:

*A message from Donald Ross greets players at the starter's desk.
(AP/WWP)*

"I sincerely believe this course to be the fairest test of championship golf I have ever designed. It is obviously the function of the championship course to present competitors with a variety of problems that will test every type of shot, which a golfer of championship ability should be qualified to play. Thus, it should call for long and accurate tee shots, accurate iron play (and I consider the ability to play the longer iron shots as the supreme test of a great golfer). Precise handling of the short game and precise putting."

— J. Donald Ross.

Least Obvious Gem

Cal Brown wrote in 1973 that "of all the famous courses, the least obvious gem is the No. 2 course at Pinehurst. It is not as dramatic as Pine Valley or Pebble Beach, not as elegant as Augusta National or Merion. Pinehurst No. 2 appears quiet, unassuming, almost drab in comparison with those American classics."

Brown points out that Ben Hogan won his first professional tournament at Pinehurst. And he defines the greatness of the course in explaining that the first three holes are a delicate and fair beginning. He adds, "The sequencing of holes of different lengths builds with a harmony and logic only achieved in great art."

I Visited a Course in Georgia Last Week ...

It was a simple mention, really an afterthought. It certainly was not meant as a comparison. John Derr, a young newspaperman, in 1935 was standing in the lobby of the country club at Pinehurst and muttered a profound, "I visited a course in Georgia last week, and it was the prettiest course that I have seen."

Derr, a rookie newspaperman, did not mention that he had covered the second Masters Championship at Augusta National. He didn't have to. He didn't mention that he was a couple of holes away from where Gene Sarazen recorded what is possibly the most historic golf shot in history—his four wood for double-eagle on the 15th hole. Derr did not even mention the name Sarazen, and the double eagle was not part of the story he was weaving. Derr wanted to describe the beautiful golf course—the playing field. Derr was not so interested in the shot. He was speaking to Mr. Wilson, the manager of the Pinehurst clubhouse. Derr wanted him to understand the quality of the course. Wilson's response was a simple, "Uh huh."

It was the response from the gentleman in the vest behind Mr. Wilson that turned the tide of the conversation. Derr, eager to get back to the photographer's convention at the hotel, was redirected by the gentleman in spectacles and a vest who stopped Derr in midsentence to explain that Pinehurst had a fine course, too.

Derr, who later became a television journalist for the Masters and other golfing events, simply stated his perception of a superb golfing venue. The man behind him was Donald Ross. He was tapping his toe, waiting for the right time to interject a statement. And his first comment was, "Come with me, and I'll show you a golf course."

Reluctantly, Derr walked around the clubhouse with his now eager tour guide. They walked around the clubhouse to the first tee where Ross sauntered down the first fairway and said, "I have grass on three greens." Bending down and showing him the first green, Ross never stopped to allow Derr a chance to steer the conversation any other direction. Instead, they went to the second hole and discussed the sand in the bunkers. Ross and Derr made it to the third hole, and Ross showed Derr the mounding and discussed the importance of the second shot into the third hole. The positioning of the tee and the contour of the fairway were parts of the script that allowed the player in harmony to maneuver to the position in which par was a possibility.

Derr endured. Finally, after a couple of hours of visiting the course, he made it back to the hotel. He was greeted by a few of his convention mates with smiles.

"Where ya been?"

"You wouldn't believe. I made a comment about my trip to Augusta to see the Masters and this man insisted on me seeing the course."

"Well, you missed the contest," said the group of photographers.

"The contest?" asked Derr.

"Yeah, we had a nude model."

Derr says, "I have never forgiven Mr. Ross for the day he wanted to show me the course."

A Little Walk in the Park

When asked to describe the Pinehurst No. 2 course, long-time director of golf Don Padgett said, "It's like a walk in the park." Padgett ushered Pinehurst into an important era in golfing history. "I came on board when I think Pinehurst was turning the corner," he once said. He was a teacher—a mentor. Padgett died in May of 2003, leaving a legacy of accomplishment in the world of golf. During the 1970s he was the director of the PGA of America. He is service at the PGA championship was widespread. Long-time colleague Ken Crow said, "We took a trip to Firestone about 10 years ago. There was Don in pictures with the champion. Then we took a trip to Pebble Beach, there was Don, again, in pictures with the champion." A young apprentice in the Golf Advantage School said, "I watched the Golf Channel and was checking out the rough condition of Augusta [it was video of an event in the 1970s] and there was Padge—a rules official. What is most amazing about the impression he made on the sport is that Padgett was an understated gentleman of the game. As an administrator, his hand was on the pulse of both the amateur and professional game.

At Pinehurst he cultivated the spirit, which eventually brought major championship golf back to the sandy soil of central North Carolina. Long-time friend and golf administrator Ken Crow said, "He did not always give you the answer. He taught you three or four ways to handle many situations, which then led you to the answer. He taught in parables." Padgett was most proud of the players who walked up the Pinehurst Country Club steps. "Anyone who is anyone in golf has had their picture taken on the brick steps at Pinehurst."

When it comes to the course around Pinehurst, his words flowed with ease. "You should never hit a ball out of bounds here, and there are no water hazards. You should finish with the same ball you started with." That really never helped golf ball sales in the pro shop. But what separates the game at No. 2 is how many times you strike the ball, especially around the greens. "They are inverted saucers. I watched Tiger Woods during a practice round at the 1999 U.S. Open. He dropped a ball behind the 18th green and started with a six or seven iron. His precision to get the ball to stop on the crest of the green was amazing with each club. That is the *way* around here," said Padgett. He admitted that there is nothing really intimidating about Pinehurst. "On the surface there is no stadium environment here. The fairways are quite wide and open. You finish your round and you say, 'Why don't I play this course better than I do?' One of the recent publications honoring No. 2 as a true classical test of golf said, 'It's a lot like listening to the recording of a symphony orchestra. Repeated listenings are needed to fully appreciate the depth of the meaning.' Golfers on Pinehurst No. 2 might need a second or third round listening to savor its timeless appeal."

After All, It's Just a Little Walk in the Park

And the players who have played at Pinehurst, well, all the world's a stage and the men and women are merely players. Padgett used to talk about the big three—meaning Nicklaus, Palmer and Trevino. All found the fairways of Pinehurst.

What makes Pinehurst No. 2 so special? Lee Trevino said, "No condominiums around it. When you look across the fairway, you can see other players. You are not looking at a big dog going woof, woof. Or there are no swimming pools in somebody's yard. You are not looking at fences and stuff. That's what makes this golf course so great. You go out there and it is quiet. All you can hear is the birds chirping. You don't see any rubber flamingos in the back yards."

Just a Scrapbook

"He was like a grandfather to me," said Sam Taylor, who worked at the Golf Advantage School in the early 1990s, referring to Don Padgett. "He was more than just a golf historian, professional and confidant to so many that worked in the golf business." At Pinehurst he was a man who steered the ship clear of the fog. Many believed he was an integral part of why, after so many years of absence, the USGA and the PGA Tour took another look at the forgotten resort.

Some thought the Carolina drought of the late 1960s, '70s and '80s was about rain and sandy soil. Others, now looking back, know it was about the neglect the Pinehurst golf courses were receiving. It turned a dogleg at the time Padgett came on board. The return of professional golf was a step in the right direction. The two tour championships in 1991 and 1992 navigated them through the thick and thin in more ways than one. Thick being the stoutly winner of the 1991 event, Craig Stadler. Thin being the subsequent year champion, Paul Azinger. Taylor says, "Until those two tournaments, some thought Pinehurst was just a resort course.

"I was learning the golf business from the inside, much like a blue-collar worker in a factory," said Taylor. Like so many who worked at Pinehurst, Taylor did not expect to get a lot of respect from the leader, the man in charge. He remembers Padgett's spirit beyond the sport. "He had a way of endearing you to the game, and with Mr. Padgett, it wasn't all about golf."

One day Padgett called Taylor into his office. Padgett's

office could have been a shrine of golf memorabilia and accomplishments. It was not. It was understated, much like the man. Taylor was certain the meeting was called to reprimand him for a task he had forgotten to accomplish the previous day. As Taylor sat down, Padgett pulled out a large scrapbook of golf-related paperwork and pictures, from Padgett's days at PGA of America and his countless hours at various clubs throughout America. Padgett kept a collection of letters and notes. On this summer day he asked Taylor to look at a letter he had received from Jack Nicklaus in 1977.

In 1977, a red-haired Huck Finn-looking Tom Watson, (10 years his junior) was beginning to make a mark on the PGA Tour. Watson beat Nicklaus in head-to-head duels at Augusta and again at the British Open. At this time, Padgett was the president of the PGA of America. He had run into Nicklaus during a difficult year. Jack approached Padgett and asked, "What do we need to do to change the format of the Ryder Cup? We need all of continental Europe to be a part of this thing," said Nicklaus. Padgett coached Nicklaus. Padgett said, "The way it works is this: one of the leading players in the game sends a letter of recommendation to me. Then, as administrator, I could then act on that letter."

Padgett soon received a letter from Nicklaus. The letter was succinct. He mentioned in the letter than it was time for the Ryder Cup to change the format and include European players. Jack Nicklaus also describes this in his autobiography, *My Story*, with Ken Bowden.

Padge, as Taylor liked to remember him, kept his scrapbook in his desk. "It had a lot of golf history. More than I had ever seen."

2

The North and South Championship

The North and South Amateur remains the longest consecutive running amateur championship in America. It began as a means to afford golfers a competitive arena and to generate publicity for a five-year-old resort. And its namesake was created to foster good relations between two geographic regions that only a generation earlier had battled each other in the Civil War. The first stroke was played at the North and South Amateur on the first day of April 1901. Henry Haynie, of the Newton Centre Golf Club in Boston, nicknamed the event one that "united the South and North Championship."

One of the highlights of the first championship was a long driving contest. The event was won with a smash of 180 yards, eight inches. Tiger Woods hits his seven iron this distance into a stiff breeze.

The women competed with the men the first couple of years of tournament play, and the Women's North and South was added in 1903. This same year, they inaugurated a North and South Open. Donald Ross claimed top prize in the Open the very first year. The following champions of the North and South Open read like a who's who in the first part of the 20th century: Walter Hagen (1918, 1923, 1924), Horton Smith (1929, 1937), Sam Snead (1949, 1950), Ben Hogan (1940, 1942) and Tommy Bolt (1951). As far as the amateur championship, Jack Nicklaus won the event in 1959, just prior to turning professional. His son won the event in 1985. Current PGA Tour players Davis Love III and Corey Pavin also hold the Putter Boy championship trophy, Love III in 1984 and Pavin in 1981. The championship did not move to the No. 2 course until 1909. In 1946, Thomas McG. Pierce, at the Vermont Amateur Championship, stood on the 11th tee, seven down to his opponent. He won the last eight holes to win his match. In 1926, a young man George Dunlap Jr. played in his first North and South Amateur as a 17-year-old. Five years later he won his first championship. He reeled off six more wins in 1933, 1934, 1935, 1936, 1940 and 1942.

North and South

The North and South Tournament is the oldest consecutive running amateur event in the United States.

In 1894, two golf clubs, Newport (RI) Golf Club and New York's St. Andrews Golf Club, held invitational golf tournaments. The winners of those two events declared themselves national champions. This prompted public outcry and was the impetus for the advent of amateur golf in America. Less than a year later, the national tournament, known as the U.S. Amateur, was born. Contested each year until 1917, the U.S. Amateur is, by one day (next to the U.S. Open), the oldest contested golf tournament in America. So, what happened in 1917? World War I. There would be no championship played the next two years.

Was golf played those two years? Was there a form of championship golf contested? There was in Pinehurst. The North and South Amateur was played each year. In 1917, Norman H. Maxwell defeated William C. Fownes Jr. two and one. In 1918, Irving S. Robeson beat Robert Stranahan in the finals 1-up.

That's not to say Pinehurst was not supportive of the war efforts. While the USGA suspended its national championships, several exhibitions were held, and select amateur events continued like the North and South, the Western and the Southern Amateur. And so, the North and South later used this continuation of play in billing itself as the oldest consecutively played amateur tournament in America.

A 16-year-old named Bobby Jones played one interesting part in the diversion from war. Jones banded with three other players, Alexa Sterling, Perry Adair and Elaine Rosenthal to form the Dixie Kids. They toured from coast to coast raising money (estimated at more than $150,000) for the Red Cross.

Amateur players Francis Ouimet and Charles Evans Jr., also made personal sojourns across the land to promote the game and aid in hometown efforts. It was in this year that Ouimet actually came under scrutiny for having worked for a sporting goods company. His amateur status was revoked, but after a series of heated discussions, Ouimet regained his amateur status.

Some golf courses were even used as gardens and grazing fields during this time of war. Other courses were used as landing strips for aircraft. And while war-time sentiment was at an all-time high, golf was really not waning. Statistics indicated during this two-year period that golfers on the 2,002 different courses in the United States spent more than $10.5 million on golf balls. A new golf ball was also introduced. The Radio golf ball was advertised as, "The Ball of Mystery that never loses life or shape due to its inherent radioactive properties."

The North and South has been criticized for not being able to find a permanent home on the golf calendar in recent years. The game will never replace the North and South, and the tradition will continue…

Amateur

Richard Tufts addressed a crowd of who's who in golf at the Southern Golf Association Banquet in 1960. His speech was emotional and charged regarding the "soft spots in the game of golf." He put the troubles with the game of golf in two categories: A love of ease and a love of money. "The game's standards are being lowered, and subtly, bit by bit, golf is losing character," he warned. He added, "Those unable to meet the challenge of the game seem to find a vicarious pleasure in destroying it." It all began in his opinion with the change in the stymie rule and the change in ball marking on the green. He was referring to changes in the match-play rule of stymie and how a ball is marked on the green in tournament play. Then, with a thunderous voice

The putting green situated near the clubhouse gives players a chance to test their roll on the challenging moss. (Photo provided by the Pinehurst Convention and Visitors Bureau.)

he declared the greatest evil of the game had become… the electric cart. How can an amateur player, fully capable of walking 18 holes, use an electric cart? This was all said with Paul Cushman, the cart manufacturer in the audience. Tufts was on quite a roll. He continued to elaborate on another contentious issue. How can we allow money to become a part of what is an amateur sport? He declared the pro circuit and its monetary influence on the games were beginning to bring the sport down. He then pointed his finger at Sam Snead for his failure to penalize himself in the recently televised 15-club incident. "Why wasn't the match stopped then and there?" asked Tufts.

In 1960, Pinehurst was headed for some lean years. Golf was beginning to change, and Tufts was adamant that the game be preserved. He insisted that the game be developed on the amateur side of the sport. This would be a major part of Tufts's legacy.

Pinehurst is Tufts personified—understated. The southern splendor does not hit you in the face, but rather oozes into your pores like the fresh pine scent.

Tufts had a lot to do with the way Pinehurst was shaped. A humble man and the grandson of founder James Tufts, he took over the direction of Pinehurst in 1930. At the age of 34, Tufts recognized the importance of the game of golf to the resort and became intrigued by its purest form—the amateur player. The club expanded its golf courses to six under his direction, and he later became instrumental in fully developing the rules of golf. An academic, Tufts was cerebral when he examined the rules of golf. He served as president of the USGA in 1956-57, and was a chief organizer in unifying the rules of the game. An accomplished player himself, Tufts said about the North and South Championship, "The mission over the years has been simple, to provide an annual gathering of those who love the game, rather than a spectacle."

The amateur game flourished from the time Francis Ouimet won the Open in 1913 to the time Bobby Jones completed his Grand Slam in 1930.

By 1951, the importance of the amateur game was waning. Following the 1951 Ryder Cup matches at Pinehurst, Tufts was so disgusted in the tide turning to the money of the professional game that he insisted that the North and South Open be abandoned after 49 playings. He said, "The PGA manual lists 88 circuit pros, and yet this small group now exerts an influence on golf which is all out of proportion to their relative importance in the *game*." He adds, "The PGA was interested in money and not prestige."

The PGA was looking after its own. Instead of offering free room and board to the professionals, they decided to add this equivalent money value to the tournament purses. Tufts was not interested in anyone lining their pockets. He was interested in the ideals of family that were set forth by his father. In his book, *The Scottish Invasion*, (a review of American golf in relation to Pinehurst and the 62nd National Amateur), Tufts held strongly to his belief:

> "It was the hope of James W. Tufts to establish Pinehurst as a small, friendly community where those in need of it could find health-giving relaxation wither for years of their retirement or for the purpose of equipping them to perform their daily tasks more efficiently…Golf came to America as the great *amateur* sport, rich with tradition and enjoying the highest possible standards of ethics and good sportsmanship in its play. The idea has been to accept the game at Pinehurst in this form and to maintain and preserve these standards in order that amateur golfers may find at Pinehurst those things which Tufts sought to provide."

William Campbell knows the role that Richard Tufts played in shaping the game of golf. "The real trinity of father figures to the game of golf was Ike Grainger, Dick Tufts and Joe Dey. Dick Tufts was an engineer, a music lover, widely read in the classics, highly educated, and had a great sense of humor. But possibly above all else, he was a man of very high standards."

William Campbell remembers the times during his declining years that he would visit Dick Tufts in Pinehurst and ask him to join him at the North and South or World Amateur Championships. "He was a proud man and really built Pinehurst, brick by brick, into a superior resort. He did not want to sell the company, I'll tell you that. He did not have majority control and they just ran out of capital," said Campbell.

Campbell sat at the 1953 Walker Cup dinner in Marion, MA. The match was played at Klittansett Club. The USGA president at the time was Totton P. Heffelfinger. Lord Brabazan concluded his pre-match words with a tribute to "Ike, Joe, Dick and Tott, the USGA's impregnable monosyllabic quadrilateral."

But he insists that the most impressionable gift Tufts left golf was his effort to take the rules of the USGA and the R&A and make them one. "Oh, I played in the British Amateur in 1950, and they handed me nine single-spaced pages of differences in the rules of the game. A lot of modern day players do not realize that," said Campbell.

This was the beginning of the end. In 1951 at Birkdale, the teams had conversations regarding the rules from the size of the golf ball, to the stymie, to the center-shafted putter.

Joe Dey, Ike Grainger and Tufts spearheaded the mission to combine the Royal and Ancient rules into what we now know as the rules of golf. It took 32 years. Tufts deserves a marked share of the credit.

In 2000, *Golfweek* devoted an entire issue to amateur golf. Richard Mudry wrote an article in the issue entitled, "Lost Luster—North and South Amateur struggles to regain its former prestige." Mudry points to issues ranging from the time of season when the event is played, to the lack of appreciation in the younger player for the historical significance of the event and the course.

Because the golf calendar has more dimples than the golf ball, the North and South has had to jockey from spring to late summer and now to mid-summer to attract the amateur players.

But as the magazine discussed the bunkers of hardship for tournaments, the overall sentiment was that the game has flourished. The amateur offerings are more in number. The likes of Carol Semple Thompson, who is a lifelong amateur, are the exception. Amateur golf is now a proving ground, a springboard. And Tufts would be proud of this: it is where the rules of the game are implemented. Scott Verplank winning the Western Open (1985) and Phil Mickelson winning the Tucson Open (1991) as amateurs are as close as we have come to a Francis Ouimet kind of experience. Since the little guy stunned Harry Vardon and Ted Ray at the 1913 U.S. Open, the game has ebbed and flowed. The Curtis Cup and Walker Cup teams are now mostly made up of the best college players.

It has definitely changed. Did America take the game too far, or did modern society take the game and turn it into big business?

At Pinehurst, a statue next to that of Donald Ross near the 18th green commemorates Richard Tufts's life. There is a sense that he would have wanted to shake the hand of every amateur golfer who finishes a round at Pinehurst.

Every amateur player should thank Richard Tufts. Every player who plays by the rules of golf should thank Richard Tufts.

Don't Listen to Wiffy Cox

If you come from Brooklyn, you'd better be tough. And Wiffy Cox wasn't a prize fighter. He wasn't the best golfer, either, because he had trouble finishing the tournaments. He had such a raging desire to win every event he played in, well, he would sometimes erupt. One sportswriter called him "a crusty professional."

In 1931, Cox showed up in Pinehurst with steel shafts on his clubs. He was a slightly built, balding man who often used salty language when things weren't going well. Cox managed to keep his mouth shut and let his steel shafted clubs do the talking in 1931. He won the North and South Open.

And in 1934, Cox was trailing Byron Nelson in his home state of Texas in the Texas Open. Nelson led through the first three rounds, and both Cox and Nelson were seeing the growth of what was known as the PGA tournament Bureau. Cox's frustration almost got the best of him when he was seen using words unknown to Texans in the third round.

But in the final round, Cox was quiet as he beat Nelson in the Texas Open in 1934.

The same year, the PGA Tournament Bureau crowned Paul Runyan as its leading money winner with a grand total of $6,767 in total earnings.

Cox also won the 1935 Agua Caliente Open in Mexico. He later became the head professional at Congressional Country Club in Bethesda, MD.

Arnold Palmer

"Back in the day when I first played Pinehurst, if your ball left the fairway, it went to the sand and then the pine needles; Not anymore…" said Arnold Palmer.

Arnold Palmer first arrived in Pinehurst in 1947 after his father discovered Pinehurst. His dad, a golf professional in Latrobe, Pennsylvania, insisted his son check out this haven for golf. Then a freshman at Wake Forest, Palmer came over during a fall break to, as he calls it, "play with dad's gang." They played the No. 2 course, and Palmer decided that the course was a magnificent test of golf. Palmer returned several times, including trips to compete in the Southern Conference Championship and the North and South. Palmer lost twice in the semifinals of the North and South, but his admiration for Pinehurst No. 2 runs deep. "Oh, it's changed over the years, but the secret to Pinehurst is to keep the putter in your hands. A lot of the greens fall off and that can be a real problem. I really think you have to take your chances and putt the ball up those slopes to the pins."

Palmer admits that some of his trips to Pinehurst for the North and South Amateur were eye-opening experiences.

"I think I got beat 11 and nine in one semifinal and five and four in the other. I lost to Stranahan and Ward."

Ben Hogan

When Ben Hogan won the North and South Open at Pinehurst in 1940, John Derr, like most daily newspaper reporters, was trying to make a deadline. Unlike in today's media climate, where stories are e-mailed and then poured electronically into the body of the paper, Derr did it all by hand.

"In those days, I had to compile the story and then also submit the headline. It was all done by the reporter, and when Ben won the North and South, he was a little bit of an unknown. Sure, he went on to win in New York, Greensboro and Asheville, but I told one of the editors to make the headline: 'Hogan's 278 wins North and South at Pinehurst.' This typically would not have been a problem, had the editor followed Derr's directions. Just prior to the paper being run for the early edition, Derr went into the press room and realized a mistake of mass proportions.

When Derr had indicated the size of the headline: he went with an eight-column head so the headline on the sports page was as bold as the morning sun. The problem was the headline read: "Hagen's 278 wins North and South at Pinehurst."

Derr sought out the editor and asked how the mistake could have been made. The editor's reply was, "I assumed it was Walter Hagen. Who the hell is Hogan?"

Stop the presses.

1984 North and South

When Joe Inman was spotted in the crowd of the 1984 North South Amateur, he was considered a celebrity. After all, the PGA professional, also a former North South champion, was returning to the grassroots level—the amateur game. It was a bright sunny day in May of 1984 when Inman declared, "I'm having a great time. I'm watching the future." And one may have deducted that Inman was referring to his brother John, a senior at North Carolina who was battling a Tarheel teammate named Davis Love III. Inman could not believe what he was watching. On the par-five fourth hole, Love knocked his second shot over the green from 210 yards away with a seven-iron. On the par-five (487-yard) eight, he hit a six-iron over the green. And he reached the par-five tenth with a drive and a one-iron. Inman said, "Nobody is as long as Davis, maybe Greg Norman."

Love won the North and South four and three. Then both Tar Heels flew to Houston to compete in the NCAA tournament. Inman must have been just warming up at Pinehurst. Inman shot a record-setting 17-under-par 271 over four days to win the individual championship. Inman still shares this record with guys named Mickelson (Arizona State, 1992) and Leonard (Texas, 1994).

Sims vs. Molder

Pinehurst has had a long-time relationship with the Bermuda Golf Association. Bermuda lacked adequate instructional programs for their junior players, so Pinehurst worked out an agreement to allow them to send some of their promising young players to Pinehurst in the summers. One young man, Michael Sims, came to Pinehurst three summers in the early '90s to learn the game. Don Padgett remembered him walking up to the North and South Amateur trophy saying, "One day my name will be up there." Sims wanted his name next to Nicklaus, Love, III, Ouimet, Pavin, Sutton, Hallberg, Strange, Patton, Stanahan, Ward, Inman and Furgol.

Before the 2001 Men's North and South, Sims was a long shot to compete for the title. He was just another college golfer playing in one of the best summer amateur events available. Sims was ignored by a lot of NCAA Division I golf schools. His resume was not dotted with a lot of achievements, so he ended up at Rhode Island University.

Bryce Molder was the antithesis of Sims. The second best recruit in the nation, he chose Georgia Tech over every other top-flight Division I school that courted him. He was a four-time All-American (only Hallberg, Mickleson and Duval did that) and won the prestigious Jack Nicklaus award as a freshman. Molder actually played in the 1999 U.S. Open with teammate Matt Kuchar. He missed the cut.

Molder grabbed a 1-up lead after the morning round. Both players finished the first 18 holes in one under on course No. 2. Sims birdied the 21st (third) and 23rd (fifth) holes to grab his first lead of the day. Molder battled back with a par on the 31st and eventually led 1-up heading into the final hole of the match. Molder's drive on 18 went left into a grove of trees. He played an excellent shot to within 20 feet of the cup. Meanwhile Sims hit an iron-shot inside Molder's. Molder's first putt hung on the lip, and the putt did not fall. Sims calmly stroked his putt to extend the match to extra holes. Pars halved the 37th, but on the next hole Molder was forced to play short of the green on his approach. His tee ball was just enough in the rough for him to not be able to advance it all the way to the green.

Sims ended up two-putting for the par and the title. Of the 31 possible matches in the 2001 North and South, 19 went extra holes. Molder was no stranger, having to play at least 17 holes in each of his matches that began on Wednesday.

Sims was able to walk in the clubhouse and have destiny served on the North and South Trophy.

The Crow's Nest

Ken Crow was 15 when his father moved the family to Pinehurst. He spent the summer picking up range balls. The next summer he got a promotion, re-gripping clubs and working inside the golf shop. He eventually went to college at Campbell University. His mind never left Pinehurst, and he returned to work at Pinehurst in the 1980s and eventually became the director of the Golf Advantage Schools. Today, Ken Crow works as the director of national sales for Pinehurst. He has arguably seen more golf over the last 30 years than anyone associated with the resort.

Crow was invited to play in the 1982 North and South Amateur. He remembers playing behind a young curly-haired young man from Southern California named Corey Pavin. Crow was playing a qualifying round on Pinehurst No. 1 when he got to the third hole, a short dogleg to the right. The third hole is typically played with an iron out to the bend in the dogleg, which leaves a short iron into the green. When he got to the green he looked back toward the tee box. He spotted a small white sphere bounding up on the green. Another kid in his group remarked, "That's that kid from Louisiana who can really bomb it." Crow remembers asking the participant the player's name.

"Hal Sutton."

Most of all, Crow knows Pinehurst, and the one word he keeps repeating as he remembers golf over the years: "heritage."

Crow remembers a young Pat Perez winning the PGA Junior event in 1995. He remembers a young Tiger Woods claiming the Big "I" Insurance Youth Classic. He remembers Davis Love and his brother Mark tagging along with dad at the *Golf Digest* schools.

"One of the most integral events ever played at Pinehurst was in 1951," insists Crow. "What happened that year was the name players that were part of the 1951 Ryder Cup did not play in the North and South Open." Crow mentions this was the impetus for the resort refusing to host another professional event for the next 20 years.

Eating dinner with Phil Mickelson a year after his runner-up finish to Payne Stewart, Crow asked the left hander about his opinion of Pinehurst. Mickelson fidgeted in his chair and said, "The course is a challenge, but I know I can play better."

Crow acknowledges the strain that the No. 2 course puts on a player, even a premium player. "The course does not demoralize you. It eats at you in a way that you are challenged. It puts pressure on so many parts of your game that often you cave in. Look at how the course held up in the 1999 Open. The course was so different than the norm that they play week in and week out on the PGA Tour that the pervading sentiment was, 'This thing is hard.'"

3

The U.S. Open

Any time a course previously hosted an event like the U.S. Open, the drama before the event centers on the course. And any time a player named Nicklaus shows up to play in the U.S. Open, the attention usually swings toward the man who has played in and had more success than any other player over the last half-century.

When the Open made its way to Pinehurst in 1999, the USGA knew Pinehurst was not a traditional U.S. Open site. But it was a traditional site. Traditional in the sense that it was an old-time classic-ground, strokes-type course. The vernacular goes something like this: straight hitter, par is a good score, great iron player—your champion.

Jack Nicklaus walked into the press room at the 1999 U.S. Open with the same confident stare that he brought to Inverness in 1957 as a 17-year-old kid playing in his first U.S. Open. He said, "I remember I was leading the tournament after three holes. I holed a 35-footer for a birdie on the first hole and I parred the next two holes—never to be seen again." Well, we know better. Nicklaus was not seen on the radar anymore that week, but he did go on to win four U.S. Opens in an 18-year span.

Forty years earlier he had visited Pinehurst and shot over 80 in his final two rounds to win the North and South. In 1959, Nicklaus was a pudgy kid from Southern Ohio with a game that held promise. He remembers the North and South as a brutal test. "The greens were as hard as rocks. If you hit the ball off line you could get in a hole or sand, and it would just bounce in a bunch of different directions. Today they work so hard to get the condition of the golf course more uniform and consistent. Some of the shots that were unfair and some of the bad shots from those days just do not happen anymore, mostly because of the technology, we have the ability to reduce the course down." The North and South is a special place for the Nicklaus family. Twenty-six years after Nicklaus claimed victory in the North and South, his son Jackie came to Pinehurst to win the title. While he was walking the fairways with Jackie that week, his son said, "This is a great golf course." Jack responded, "This isn't just a great golf course, it's a fabulous test of golf." He adds in modern terms, "Any course that does not have water hazards and does not have a tree that comes in play for the entire round, but still tests every facet of your game is a wonderful test of golf."

And Nicklaus the designer knows the intricacies that make a good golf course great and a great golf course a possible venue for a major. He said on the eve of the 1999 championship, "Donald Ross got the contour of the land to move in a natural rustic way with the length needed to provide a great challenge."

The competitive Nicklaus knows a little about the mental edge needed to play the course and the championship. "I used to love to listen to players gripe. The rough is too high: check him off. The greens are too fast: check him off. You just check guys off as they complain, because they complain themselves right out of the championship."

And as a living designer of golf courses, he knows the difference between complaining and criticism. "The only difference between Pinehurst and many other courses is the shaving off of the greens. Between Augusta and Pinehurst there are a lot of similarities. Let me just say that these are the smallest-playing large greens, good-sized greens that I've ever seen." And Nicklaus adds, "You can get away with that, because Donald Ross is no longer around."

A living designer, Nicklaus knows that the perception of U.S. Open courses is skewed. "If you look at most of the golf courses that the U.S. Open is played on, the only difference is the trees. And I think that is ridiculous criteria for what's a good golf course. Whether the tree is 10 years old or 50 years old should not matter."

The pine at Pinehurst has been around a while. And with a generous width of the fairways, the only penalty seems to be the errant shot.

Ross still receives kudos for his subtle design characteristics—the grass bunkers around the greens, the slopes, angles and lie difficulties. They all pose threats to the player from yesterday and today.

USGA tournament agronomist Tim Morgahan worked with Paul Jett and his staff prior to the 1999 U.S. Open to get the course in tournament condition. Was it a fair U.S. Open test? It really began somewhere just after the 1994 U.S. Senior Open in 1994. Brad Kocher, Bob Farren and Paul Jett re-built the putting greens. It was all of that and more, otherwise the USGA would not have responded by spinning the event back to Pinehurst in 2005. Morgahan is usually one of the first to the U.S. Open site to prepare the course, greens, tees, fairways, roughs, and bunkers, for play. Moraghan knew that at Pinehurst, the word rough was going to be similar to what rough is at Augusta—not part of the equation. But in 1999, the rough was a factor. It provided an interesting twist to the outcome, with Payne Stewart playing short of the 72nd hole.

"What defines greatness?" ponders Jim Moraghan. "Just walk outside the door here. It's an outstanding golf course. And I don't care if it's 1940, 1990 or 2030; I think it's going to hold up. Even with the advancements in turf grass, in agronomic equipment, and with players' equipment, you still have to make the golf shot. And Ross was no dummy, and he knew what he was doing, as any great architect did and will do; it's a great challenge to any player of any era."

"If we dropped out of the top 10, you bet the people around here would let us know about it," said Paul Jett, greens superintendent of Pinehurst No. 2 (on staying ranked as one of the top classical courses in America).

Pinehurst No. 2 played like a parking lot in the 1970s. The greens were like rocks according to the premier player in the game, Jack Nicklaus. Pine needles and hard, sandy soil was the only thing between the fairway and the trees. There was no rough. Not anymore. Current greens superintendent Paul Jett came aboard in 1995 to prepare the course for its first U.S. Open. The USGA met with Jett and discussed the alterations needed to make the current game part of the old playground. He was all about making the playground playable. Jett knows that Donald Ross did not have the irrigation system that exists now, and he knows that the game the Scots brought to America was not as much about the playground. That has changed. Now, the USGA and the Open venue team years in advance to get it right. They discuss the widths of the fairways, the slopes in the greens and the elevation of tee boxes. A lot of the decision to bring the U.S. Open to Pinehurst in 1999 was predicated on the agreement that the No. 2 greens would be rebuilt. "It was a two-month process in terms of the time we put a hole in the ground to the time we added the seed," said Jett. He adds, "Despite the need to cover the greens from two hurricanes, it went smooth from start to finish."

Pinehurst No. 2 has been tinkered with over the years. The greens were resurfaced in 1987, prior to the 1990 and 1991 PGA Tour Championships. And the game has changed with the technology of turf grass equipment.

What the USGA has communicated to Jett about a return of the U.S. Open has dealt with mostly more of the same. "We can't really plan for a certain kind of weather, but we can prepare," he said. "The most noticeable difference in the course in 2005 will be the fairway bunkers. Certain holes will have some fairway obstacles for players to contend with." Before play began in 1999, the back of the eighth green raised a lot of conversation. Players were bumping the ball up to the green with 3-woods, 3-irons and even wedges. They changed the mowing pattern for the area around the green, and it had a distinct effect on how the players attacked the hole.

Jett seemed to echo Moraghan's agronomistic approach to the Pinehurst legacy of championship golf. "I think this course will stand for a long time just because of the greens. Nobody is going to get scared playing this golf course from tee to fairway. But, because with the penalty of a bad iron shot from the fairway into the green, I believe this course will stand for many, many years," Jett said.

And players like Olazabal were mentioned in the pre-tournament hype, based on the fact that the Pinehurst layout represents what a lot of European players are used to: skin-tight lies around the green, generous landing areas for drives and a premium on the short game. "I think Pinehurst is very similar to what they will encounter on the other side of the ocean. I think that was Ross's intention when he came over here," said Moraghan prior to play. And in 1999, it just so happened that Olazabal was the only player to have a chance at the Grand Slam having won the Masters a few months prior. "Maybe the way the golf courses have been set up in Europe, it allows us to use our imagination. We could run the ball, bounce it 20, 30 yards short of the green and run it onto the green. We are used to playing in bad weather conditions."

The Grand Slam

Jose Maria Olazabal came into the 1999 U.S. Open as the only player to have a chance to win the Grand Slam. The spectacular short game player and Masters Champion had the game to give the No. 2 course a run for the second leg of the Grand Slam. He also had a sense of humor heading to Pinehurst. Asked before the tournament what his greatest assest was, his head or his heart. His reply? "My nose. Look at it."

When Olazabal got down to playing the Ross layout, he was able to farm out a 70-75. On Friday, a birdie on 11 made him one over for the championship. This was the beginning of the end. He bogeyed 13, 15, 17 and struggled to a double bogey on the 18th hole on Friday. The back nine 38 prevented him from playing golf on Saturday and Sunday, but it did not prevent the frustration inside the Masters Champion's soul. He proceeded to the men's locker room where he punched a wall and broke his hand. Olazabal would indeed win the grand slam award in 1999, just not for winning golf's four majors.

Behind the Scenes

Reg Jones, member of the U.S. Open executive committee, reflected on the 1999 U.S. Open.

"We had perfect beer weather, but as far as the rain, we had an over-supply of water." Pinehurst, which hosted the club pro championship in 1998, learned the hard way. The balmy conditions with temperatures escalating over 100 produced health issues, including several cases of heat stroke. The tournament committee, wary of the severity of the heat, remembers the plan for the Open. "We were going to have more water than we would need." He added, "We finished the tournament with more water than we needed, but a lack of wind shirts."

Jones remembers that the wet and rainy conditions necessitated a little last-minute strategical planning. The Harness race track served as the Pinehurst bus depot. Several buses were under contract to transport people to various drop-off points on the golf course. The Wednesday night rain before the first round of the 1999 Open left the bus depot in a quagmire. The local army corps of engineers provided special platelets to preserve the surface. The rain intensified so that most of the platelets were washed away. This left a large two-foot hole and a decision to reconfigure the entire transportation system. A local contractor came to the rescue, grading the area and filling it with gravel. The last roller was moving through as the first bus was leaving to run their first shuttle. "Timing was too perfect," remembers Jones.

The Prodigal Son

The 1998 U.S. Open was played at San Francisco's Olympic Club. Lee Janzen claimed the trophy. Payne Stewart finished second.

The USGA, which likes to sit perched in the shadows, is the governing body of the nation's championship, which likes the rough and the scores high.

As in baseball, tennis and basketball, the umpires, referees and line judges provide the proper rulings so that the focus is on the athlete competing within the guidelines. Golf vexes the minds of the players because of the arena. Each year, the Open championship arrives at a little venue that is usually described as "a grand old course." It becomes a lot different from a tennis court, a baseball diamond or the basketball hardwood. Golf becomes a mercurial playground, especially when the governing body decides to tinker with the edge of the abyss.

The USGA usually says that it wants to create a stern test so that it can "identify the best players." It starts with the setup of each hole: tee markers, rough height and pin placement. Mention to anyone at the USGA the two words "pinnable green," and they will jettison into a rhetorical outburst with adjectives like gnarly and wicked, and the players counter with adjectives like unfair and preposterous. Eyebrows are raised.

But when the rules official makes the headlines, then America's championship has crossed the line. That is even before any one of the players whines. Here is the nation's best golf course, and here is the 18th hole at the Escondido Putt-Putt. The difference between a no-call and a foul is one large finger pointed at the antagonist. Enter Tom Meeks, the USGA rules official, who somehow managed to allow a pin to be placed on a severe slope at the back of the 18th green in the second round at the Olympic Club. Some players could not dare mention what they were saying in the locker room. Some know the penalty about talking about the conditions. The NBA won't tolerate coaches complaining about officiating. Why not consider the same on the PGA Tour? In 1998, It reached a boiling point.

In the first round, Stewart's second shot on 18 settled to within 10 feet of the pin. His next putt was from 25 feet. He could hardly contain the fire brooding inside. "Whenever you start seeing the balls roll up to the hole and then roll back away from the hole, I think that is bordering on the ridiculous. I think that that becomes almost—I don't know if the USGA would use the term—'an illegal pin.'"

Asked if he would get a free round if he made the first putt, Stewart said, "I was watching the putt-putt championships this morning before I came out. And it resembled that hole a lot."

The Man in the Black Hat Was Tom Meeks

In contention on Sunday, the man in the black hat and the man in the plus fours had another duel. Recanting his round, when he got to how he played the 12th hole he hesitated: "I hit the fairway on 12, but I was in the bunker. I was right in the middle of a sand divot, and didn't play a very good shot."

Meeks approached Stewart after the 12th hole and said, "You got a bad time." And Stewart asked politely, "What happens if I get another one?" Meeks said, "That's a one-stroke penalty."

Forget the back left pin on 18 in the second round. Forget the sand divot in the middle of the fairway in 12. Forget the bad time from Meeks. Stewart admittedly did not play well enough to win the 1998 U.S. Open. "I guess I bring out the best in Lee Janzen," he quipped. Where was Stewart's bravado? Where was the Stewart who would let a loss like this fester in the form of a snapped five-iron? "And today was just a little bit off. And in the game of golf, a little bit can be just enough." Hmmm.

Payne Stewart was at the press conference that awarded him second place, and it seemed to be, well, not Payne Stewart. Where is the Payne Stewart who turns sour when he loses, stomps around and whines about the hand he was dealt? One reporter asked him about his legacy being tarnished. His response, "My legacy? I never knew I had one. By golly, what is my legacy? And then, I'll know if it's going to affect it or not."

The inner Payne Stewart was more mature. No tantrums, high blood pressure or snarl. Not this time. "I think the reason why I'm here, and I think the reason why you're viewing me differently, is I think I've matured and I understand what this job is about. I understand what playing golf for a living is all about and how I'm supposed to handle myself." He talked all the way to the 1999 U.S. Open.

He put himself in position to make the putt on 18 to push the event to a playoff. He and Janzen had both won a U.S. Open before. He said, "It needed to be higher and it needed to be harder. I felt like I chose the proper line, but I obviously didn't have the speed."

Meeks and Stewart. Stewart and Meeks. The red-hot embers cooled in Stewart. The contemplative anxiety swirled in Meeks. It was March of 1999 when the two met up at a rules seminar in Orlando—two men, having a burger and playing nine holes. Meeks apologized for the back left pin placement on Friday. He said, "It's the first time I've gone against my better judgment." Stewart said at the time, "That's all I needed to hear." Stewart still disagrees with certain USGA policy. Stewart challenged Meeks on being timed during the closing rounds of a major. He frowned on pairings in U.S. Opens. Now, it was the mature Stewart standing tall and taking it all in stride. "That's why there is chocolate and vanilla ice cream. "The old Stewart would not have said that. Meeks liked to chide Stewart by telling him he needed to play a little faster and work on hitting out of sand-filled divots.

Pressure. U.S. Open pressure is something Stewart learned about long ago. "Pressure, sure I'm human. But, I think I'm better dealing with it than in the past. Say at Shinnecok when Raymond (Floyd) won. I didn't understand. I wasn't prepared. Before the tournament began he said, "I didn't execute the shots last year on Sunday that I did earlier in the week. So hopefully, I'd love to have that same situation again this year."

Stewart showed up at Pinehurst as the same fun-loving player he had been throughout his career. And he was one year removed from the Olympic Club. But, as Shakespeare said, "All the world's a stage and all the men and women merely players," he must not have been looking at Stewart. He was the perfect protaganist at Pinehurst. The Scottish knickers, the fun-loving character was cast for the starring role.

Before the tournament began he said, "You are going to watch us perform this week, and you are going to see us in a totally different light than you're used to seeing us in the U.S. Open. This is a golf course that wants to make you think: 'Oh boy, I've got it in the rough, and now I'm going to whip it up on the green.' And that's where all the excitement begins. This is a golf course where you will really have to think about where you want to be. And if it gets hard, firm, fast, wow it will really be exciting."

The swagger was in place. The former U.S. Open champ had beaten Scott Simpson at Hazeltine in 1991. He knew what it felt like to be the nation's champion. And in 1991, he played in a red, white and blue ensemble. Stewart wore the knickers and the tam o'shanter, and was good enough (75) to Simpson's 77 to earn the title.

On Thursday, June 15, 1999, Stewart said it would take "red numbers" to win. Missing the cut in Memphis was maybe the beginning of Stewart's good fortune at Pinehurst. He showed up early, playing a practice round with Scott Hoch, ESPN's Jimmy Roberts and swing coach Chuck Cook. Hoch remembers Stewart and his caddy, Mike Hicks, making extensive notes on the Pinehurst No. 2. Course. They went through each hole like it was the pivotal hole in the championship, said Hoch.

Stewart showed up with an attitude that made the Olympic Club experience an afterthought. His devotion to Jesus Christ was evident in a "WWJD" bracelet his son Aaron had given to him. He wore the bracelet throughout his week at Pinehurst, and it was in full display at the awards ceremony.

A year prior, he made a statement regarding his newfound faith. "All of a sudden, golf isn't everything in my life. I have a beautiful family. If, on the way home, something would happen, and I can't play golf again, hey, I've had a wonderful career, but I want to be able to spend the rest of my life with my family and give them all the love that I can. That's one thing that Paul Azinger taught me. Golf isn't everything. God's going to call us sometime. I'm going to a special place when I die, but I want to make sure that my life is special while I'm here."

When Azinger was diagnosed with cancer, it was an awakening for Stewart. Here was a person who was one of his best friends, stricken by a disease that also took his father. This was a double-bogey in his life. He could have pity for himself and for Zinger, or he could pull himself to a higher level. It didn't happen overnight, but eventually, he decided that the "poor me" attitude was not going to make any difference. He turned his life to Jesus Christ, and he matured to a level noticed by many. Jim Nantz, who had seen Stewart from his college days, through most of his days on the PGA Tour said, "I noticed a peacefulness to him." Payne also became active in Bible study at his church. When he returned to Isleworth after the U.S. Open, he explained to the assistant pastor at his church, J.B. Collingsworth, that the reason for his success at Pinehurst was Jesus. Pointing to his bracelet, he said, "It was him."

When Stewart saw the need for something, he never held back. Before the Ryder Cup at Brookline, he made an odd request to Ben Crenshaw. "I think we need something at Brookline to let the steam out. Let us all relax." Crenshaw asked, "What would that be?" Stewart's response, "A ping-pong table."

One of the highlights of Brookline off the course, was, "who beat who" at ping-pong. The mastermind behind the entire table tennis diversion—Payne Stewart.

Whether it was wearing hot pepper pants, playing ping-pong, or setting his boat on fire in his garage: Stewart found humor in even the most serious game. He found a way to make the game less important. Sure, he was all for show-manship, after all, his early days' marketing scheme was to set him apart. The moment in time he had at Pinehurst began with a spaghetti dinner he whipped up on Wednesday, and ended with a 15-foot putt. The week was the true defining spirit of a man who had learned to manage a championship golf course, the elements and the pressure of a major.

Teacher and Pupil

It was Sunday of the U.S. Open, and Stewart was hitting balls on Maniac Hill. Harvie Ward's wife, Joanne, encouraged the former teacher to go up and renew his acquaintance with his former prize student (Stewart). Reluctantly, Ward finally walked up as Stewart sent a pull hook into the left side of the range. "I never taught you to hit that shot." Ward and Stewart embraced as the rain fell moments before Stewart teed off in the fourth round of the 1999 U.S. Open.

From a distance, Ward witnessed a transformation in his pupil. "Over the last couple of years his whole attitude changed. He was more at ease with himself. He had grown up and knew his inner self better than ever before, whereas before he was flippant and brash, because he knew he was good...He became a man instead of a boy," said Ward.

He remembers the Stewart who at times was impatient with his golf swing. "The times he got in trouble were from over-swinging on his back swing, particularly with his driver. As far as us breaking up—we were talking one time and he always wanted to move the golf ball. I said OK, but my advice to him was, 'Payne, what you've got to do is have one swing that you can depend on. Because, when you get to the last hole at the Masters or the Open, you've got to know that you can put that swing on it and know where it's going. If you're more concerned with fading it and drawing it, that might jump up and bite you someday.'"

Ward and Stewart broke off their relationship shortly after that meeting. Ward said, "Evidently he didn't like that. That was the only time we had any disagreement."

On the Outside Looking In

Phil, Tiger and David Duval were the competitors sparring with Payne Stewart on Father's Day in 1999. It just happened to be the U.S. Open. Phil, David and Tiger were members of the upcoming Ryder Cup team at Brookline, and Stewart looked at the Open as a chance to "take care of unfinished business." He was on the outside looking in.

Stewart played in Memphis the week prior to the Open and missed the cut. He said he was walking the course the Saturday before the tournament when he realized that "I was ready to play well. I took an eight-iron, nine-iron and pitching wedge and just walked the course. I came to think that the reason I didn't play well in Memphis was because I was thinking ahead to this week."

When the week ended after Stewart made the unforgettable 15-foot breaker up the hill on 18, Stewart had taken care of business. One under par won the golf tournament. All week the players and the USGA commiserated that this U.S. Open test was up to par. "Even par wins the golf tournament."

Many thought even par would make it into a playoff on Monday. As his putt curled in, Stewart drew the line. One red number one on the scoring stanchion was where he separated himself from the field. In the village of Pinehurst, the scoring differential sits on replica stanchions.

Thursday night after the first round of play, Stewart visited the Pine Crest Inn, the reputable watering hole. It was the same watering hole, where years earlier at the 1991 tour championship, he left his signature in the famed men's bathroom. It was a couple of months before the tour championship when Stewart beat Scott Simpson to win his first major, the U.S. Open at Hazeltine.

"Where's my signature I signed in 1991?" he asked the staff. The place needed a fresh coat of wallpaper a few years earlier, they said. Stewart's night at the Pine Crest was punctuated when he walked into the men's bathroom and scripted his signature just above the door. The Thursday night visitor became the Sunday night champion.

People can't forget that a year earlier Stewart had battled Lee Janzen down to the wire before losing at the Olympic Club. This time, Stewart said all the right things and made all the right putts. When he was crowned he admitted, "What happened last year was what I didn't want to hear today. When I got back to Orlando and all my friends came up and said, boy, you sure tried hard. It was a great effort. I didn't want to hear that, and that motivated me. I mean, the Ryder Cup—I've contended all year long, and the Ryder Cup's motivated me. That's one cup that isn't sitting on this table right now. It's on the wrong side of the ocean. And 300 points (the amount alloted to the Open Champion) will put me up to 917, thank you very much, and I will be on the team."

The Rolly Trinity

Three putts. Three holes. It started on 16 and ended on 18. "You just don't make three putts like that on the last three holes of a major championship like that," said Johnny Miller. He made the putts because his wife told him to keep his head down. He made the putts because his father told his wife to always remind Payne to keep his head down.

It may have started long before Stewart won the Quad Cities Open with his father watching. It started long before the 1991 Open at Hazeltine. Stewart was destined to win the 1999 U.S. Open at Pinehurst.

His legacy. His legacy is all over Pinehurst. The history, the heritage? He just added to it.

Looking back on Stewart's life as a golfer and a person is one way to remember his mark. Paul Jett watched Stewart make the putts like everyone else and now says, "The only other place he could make putts like these is in heaven."

The Father

Phil Mickelson won everything in junior golf. He claimed the NCAA championship as a freshman at Arizona State, picked up the U.S. Amateur at Cherry Hills and, for good measure, scooped a PGA Tour win before he picked up his diploma. All in good measure.

He showed up on the PGA Tour with a game fit for a king. Only it wasn't a lion, but rather a tiger, who busted his party. The lefty was supposed to win at Pinehurst in 1999.

His WWJD bracelet, a modified jacket and a love for the top prize.

His wife was about to give birth to the couple's first child, and it was Father's Day. Not to mention, he had the best short game in the universe. Convex greens, the best flop shot on the planet and a last trimester were the makings of a great story.

And if Mickelson showed up at Pinehurst, the village would address him with condolensces. That's because Payne Stewart is the adorned Mayor emeritus of the Village. There are reminders everywhere that he was the one who finished one stroke ahead of the father-to-be. His name has a red number next to it on the scoring stanchion souvenirs still sold in the Village. Stewart wore the knickers, just like the Scottish ancestors who showed up to introduce golf to America 100 years ago—at Pinehurst. Mickelson was the San Diego dude with the flipped-up collar and the flip wedge.

The 1999 U.S. Open was a cruel reminder that sometimes golf mirrors life. And it was about a progression of Stewart's tough luck at the Olympic Club the year prior. It was about a destiny (of perhaps, a higher power) that perhaps allowed the event to unfold on the 18th green on a rainy June day that year.

The Mentor

To fully understand the 1999 U.S. Open, the golfing historian has to turn the clock back one year to the Lake Course at the Olympic Club in 1998. What did Lee Janzen, the mentor, do at the Olympic Club, to prepare Mr. Stewart, the student, for Pinehurst?

Lee Janzen opened at Olympic Club with a 73, seven strokes behind leader Payne Stewart (66). But this was the U.S. Open and Janzen had the courage, or maybe the patience, to persevere. Anything can happen in an Open.

"Prior to Olympic, I really started to wonder if I was really that good, or just really lucky," said Janzen.

In the second round, Janzen played off his first day miscues to record the best round of the day (66). Stewart hung on to the lead within one stroke of Bob Tway and Jeff Maggert. This was starting to look eerily familiar to 1993 when Janzen and Stewart went head to head at Baltusrol. After two rounds, Stewart and Janzen were separated by just two strokes. On day three Stewart charged to a 70 in the windless conditions. The Olympic Club was missing some of its teeth; the San Francisco weather was not what the USGA expected.

So the stage was set for Stewart to claim his second U.S. Open since he won at Hazeltine in 1991. All that he needed was a decent round on Sunday. Stewart did not get a decent round, he scored a 74. What happened on Sunday had a lot to do with major pressure in a major championship. Janzen was seven strokes off the lead with 15 holes to play. And when he got to the fifth hole, Janzen's dreams were fading into black numbers. His attempt to play safe with a 4-wood backfired. His tee shot went into trees on the right side of the fairway. When he arrived at the landing area, he realized his ball was still up in the tree. Finally, a San Francisco breeze sent Janzen's ball to the depths of the rough. "I went from being lucky to make double-bogey to walking away with par," said Janzen. Janzen's final-round

68 nipped Stewart by a stroke and left the teary-eyed Janzen holding the prize—his second U.S. Open.

Payne Stewart, once considered a selfish, knickers-wearing Adonis, was complimented by Janzen, "I was beaten by a great round of golf." It was a gutsy round of golf by Janzen. Twenty-eight putts on a Sunday for a major is guts. Stewart said that he knew Janzen showed the game and the guts to win the year prior.

Janzen prepared with a mindful approach at Pinehurst. He said, "I love the U.S. Open. It's a major championship on one of the great courses we have in the country. I do get excited about it, and I know that because the course is so tough, it eliminates a lot of players."

Many people forget that the defending champion at the 1999 U.S. Open was Lee Janzen. His steady play made him a favorite on every Open course, and Pinehurst was no different.

"At Pinehurst, because the rough is so low, it tempts you to make a shot you wouldn't normally be trying to make. Because of that, you'll see some birdies and some doubles. If the rough was deeper, you'd see more pars and bogeys." Janzen said.

A slow-start 74-73, left the defending champion playing for respect. It was the guy who finished second to him a year prior who made the putts. It was an experienced Stewart who knew when to charge and when to sit back in the saddle and smell the pines.

One year older, one year wiser, one year smarter—Payne Stewart was the U.S. Open Champion.

Davis Love III

Davis Love has the long, smooth swing. It's the kind of silky reflex approaching the ball that could be put to music. The extension of his arms away from his body allows for maximum clubhead through impact. As a young man growing up in a golfing family, Love III was not just in Carolina in his mind. Many summers were spent tagging along with Dad to the *Golf Digest* schools, which meant an annual stop in Pinehurst.

Love said, "I can remember listening to Jack Lumpkin tell me how to pitch the ball from one of the deep greenside holes near the 15th green, so that I could get the ball up in the air." And while he learned the game on the fairways at Pinehurst, mostly the No. 4 Course, it has been a love affair that goes beyond the game. "Growing up, Pinehurst was my favorite place to come. And with the U.S. Open returning to the area, it's just special, because a lot of my friends come in town, and I can go to the Pine Crest and the Carolina Hotel and that is where my sentiment comes into play."

Love III also recalls a personal triumph on Pinehurst No. 2. "I know I won the long drive on the 14th hole." When asked how far his ball traveled, he said, "Longer than everybody else." His caddie during his amateur days, Jeff Ferguson, remembers the human one-iron's game. "He was tall and thin, but he could move the ball long and straighter than ever."

Years earlier, it wasn't really a dream for Love to play in the U.S. Open at Pinehurst. "The truth is that I dreamed of hopefully being good enough to play in the North and South one day. Just hoping I would get in the North and South was a dream. Because growing up in Georgia, I really only lived in North Carolina one year, the North and South was the biggest tournament that I could ever imagine playing."

Love III finished in a tie for 12th (70-73-74-72) at the 1999 U.S. Open after being picked by *Golf Digest* to win the event.

Curtis Strange

"We played at Pinehurst in the North and South Amateurs, Pinehurst Intercollegiates, and in June 1977 I qualified for the PGA Tour at Pinehurst. I love it. I love everything about it," said former Demon Deacon Curtis Strange (1974-1976) on Pinehurst No. 2.

When you say back-to-back U.S. Opens, the name Curtis Strange enters the conversation. In 1988 and 1989, Strange managed a repeat performance that still stands as the golfer's greatest accomplishment. But Strange, the captain of the U.S. Ryder Cup effort in 2002, is a match-play enthusiast. When you ask Strange about back to back, you expect to hear about Brookline and Oak Hill or his two national championships at Wake Forest. Not so fast.

What about the time he beat George Burns (two-up) and Fred Ridley (six and five) in the North and South Amateur?

"The North and South was huge when I played in it in 1975 and 1976. I birdied the 15th to go 1-up, and it put a stake in George's heart. That was fun," said Strange. Strange also walked the Pinehurst fairways in 1977 to gain entrance to the PGA Tour.

Arriving for the 1999 U.S. Open, Strange admitted to being absent from the grounds since the 1981 tour championship. But his sentiment for the course did not waver.

"It's one of my favorite courses. There is no rough around the greens and it's just going to be fun to have the players hit different shots. They will need a lot of imagination, and it will be interesting, because they will not be just taking out a sand wedge."

Strange was just one Wake Forest player to play at Pinehurst. A list includes: Scott Hoch, Jay Haas, Len Mattiace, Billy Andrade, Gary Hallberg, and Lanny Wadkins. And this was just the boys from one ACC school. Duke, Carolina and N.C. State also found a way to road trip to Pinehurst.

The Open Comes to Town

The Open was coming to town! The Open was coming to town! For a small village in North Carolina to receive an invitation to host the U.S. Open was like turning Mayberry into Washington D.C. for a week. Some Pinehurst capitalists saw it as an opportunity. The Pine Crest had long been regarded as the main watering hole, but they wanted something different. And so, Dugan's, an Irish Pub located appropriately at No. 2 Market Square, was opened.

Pinehurst businesses braced for what was going to be the biggest single event to hit the town. Alan Riley, a schoolteacher from Fayetteville was called and asked to help. Riley responded. The Open came, and he ran the basement bar like he owned the place, serving the Open patrons and even some of the players. One of the patrons whom Riley met up with was a little kid running around. It happened to be the grandson of the owner. By dinner that same night of the 1999 U.S. Open, the grandson offered some sage advice to his granddad, "I don't know who that guy is downstairs, but you ought to have him run your restaurant."

Riley owned a bed and breakfast/Irish pub in Spicer, Minnesota before heading to Fayetteville, NC to be a schoolteacher.

"I guess by doing a friend a favor during the 1999 Open, it was meant for me to work here." Riley left his teaching job to become an entrepreneur for the second time. Since 1999, Riley has been the whirling dervish around the Irish Pub, making sure the kegs and patrons are full.

Riley figures he is not yet considered an insider. "You have to live in Pinehurst 15 or 20 years before they consider you a local. So I am still an outsider."

Riley admits he has had some influential guests, including Payne Stewart the night before and after he won the U.S. Open, but he shrugs off the notion that it's all that important. Riley's opinion on what happens at his pub is simple: "If your food is good, your restaurant is just like your home."

For Dugan's, the 1999 U.S. Open was a start. And it is quickly getting a reputation as a 19th, 20th or 92nd hole. But math is important at Pinehurst only if you're keeping score.

John Daly

"I'm going to eat about six cheeseburgers at McDonald's, probably have a bag of Oreos and a big thing of milk, watch Sports Center *and hopefully see myself on TV," John Daly said after shooting an opening-round 68 that left him one stroke off the lead in the 1999 U.S. Open.*

With John Daly, it's a lot like beauty and the beast. When his scores are low, his patience is as old as time. In his opening round of the 1999 U.S. Open, Daly birdied the first three holes on his way to carding a 68. "I was about as much in shock as everybody else," he said. For Daly, this was the inhale. His waywardness is like the weather. "This thing with me, I don't know who is showing up tomorrow, that's the way the year has been. And it's a little scary. But I just kind of want to soak this day in and pat myself on the back for a good round that I much needed for myself and my self-esteem."

And when Daly arrived in Pinehurst in mid-June, the hurricane season was still a couple months away. That didn't matter. He followed the 68 with a second-round 77. He made the cut, but the weather was brewing. Conditions were much worse on the course and in his mind.

By Sunday Daly was out of contention, and he incurred a two-stroke penalty on the eighth hole for hitting his ball while it was still moving. This was after his previous two putts up the fringe had reached the green and been fairly close to the hole, but they slid off the crown. So, Daly knocked his ball back toward the fairway. A chip and two putts later Daly scored an 11 on the eighth. Winds of change, seasons of change, here comes the beast. After Daly turned in his scorecard which was a 13-over-par 83, he commented to NBC sports, "Yeah it's frustrating and I lost my patience. But they have too many unfair pins. It's frustrating. The U.S. Open is not John Daly's style of golf. I'm not going to Pebble Beach next year and watch the USGA ruin that golf course, too."

He said he was taking the two-stroke penalty on eight for his brothers on the PGA Tour. "I needed to stand up for the guys," he added. His playing partner, Tom Kite, had a different interpretation of the action. "Everybody has a breaking point, and John just reached his."

The former PGA and British Open Champion shot rounds of 81-83 on Saturday and Sunday. His parting shots were left for reporters within earshot as he slammed his trunk.

"I don't mind hitting the ball bad, but when I feel like I've hit the ball pretty good for four days and shoot an 81, it's not golf. It's crazy." He added, "I don't consider the U.S. Open a major anymore."

Two weeks prior to Pinehurst, Daly was playing the 18th at the Memorial in the first round. He was staring at making bogey from six feet. He ended up six-putting to record a 10 on the hole, including a field hockey jab three times to complete an opening-stanza 82. He did not sign his scorecard or say goodbye to Jack Nicklaus when he withdrew.

Tiger Woods

"He ranks right up there. I have always loved traditional courses. To me, it's the ultimate… Donald Ross ranks right up there as one of my favorites," Woods said of Pinehurst No. 2.

Never at a loss for words, Tiger Woods knew going into the final round of the 1999 U.S. Open that he still had a chance. "My game plan was to just hit fairways and greens. I hit a lot of greens today, the ball just didn't stay on them, but I hit them," he joked.

Woods made double bogey, bogey, par and birdie on the first four holes of his third round. As he looked back on the tournament, the third round was what left him just out of the Mickelson-Stewart battle on Sunday.

Woods created quite a stir when he began using the flat-faced 3-wood as a greenside chipper. "My putter has four degrees loft vs. my 3-wood, which has 15. Because my 3-wood has more loft, it enables me to put the ball on top of the grass faster and get it running, especially when I've got grain to deal with. And at Pinehurst you do. You don't get a chance to use the club around the greens unless you play a links course in Europe," Woods said.

During the 1999 event, Woods was defending his dad for snap-hook remarks about Scotland and showed concern over some pin positions. After shooting 68 in the opening round he quipped, "Did you see some of those pins? I think five was kind of borderline." He added, "Just go out there and look at them. They're right on a knob."

Whether Woods had a crystal ball is open for debate. On the final day of the 1999 U.S. Open he said, "You know this golf tournament is one I've always wanted to win, because I won three U.S. Juniors, three U.S. Amateurs, and it would be nice to win three U.S. Opens. That would be pretty neat to do. And I had a good chance this week, but it proves to me that I will definitely win a U.S. Open."

Woods owned the U.S. Open at Pebble Beach in 2000. He claimed his second U.S. Open at Bethpage Black in 2002. Will Pinehurst No. 2 be No. 3? In 1999, Woods shot a final-round 70. He was just too far back to make a run. "I didn't make one mental mistake. I made the physical mistakes. And that's part of it."

Woods said, "I think [Pinehurst] proved it was a championship golf course. This tests every single part of your game. And it was great to see. The guys are basically just off the green, making doubles. You don't see that very often, and especially when they have a chance to putt it, bump-and-run it and a whole bunch of different options, and they're still making a bunch of mistakes."

The rest of the field was not as enthusiastic about the test Pinehurst provided. But Woods has always seen Pinehurst as a place where he can win.

What a lot of golf fans don't recall is that Woods was ranked No. 2 in the world heading into Pinehurst, just behind David Duval. He was coming off a two-stroke win at the Memorial Tournament two weeks prior to the Open. And in Dublin, Ohio, it was Woods's short game that was on display. Actually, Woods made a trip to Pinehurst before heading to Jack's tournament. And he tuned up for Muirfield fresh off a convex green experience at Pinehurst.

A Tiger in the Pines at the 1999 U.S. Open. (Photo provided by the Pinehurst Convention and Visitors Bureau.)

Dave Shedloski of *Golfweek* said, "Woods was spraying the ball over the yard in the final round of the Memorial Tournament, putting him in precarious positions and pulling off one miraculous recovery after another, in effect winning Jack Nicklaus's shindig playing like Arnold Palmer."

And while Tiger was a favorite at Pinehurst in 1999, some surprising names were struggling to qualify for the event.

David Toms had to shoot 64-63 at a sectional qualifier in Germantown, Tennessee. to make the field. Other Tour players such as Chris Smith, Jay Haas, Len Mattiace, Kirk Triplett and Craig Parry had to work their way into the field, too.

After all, the word Open is like the word American. It conjures up the feeling that if the player has a heart to compete, the opportunity exists. Steve Jones in 1996 is a perfect example. Struggling with injury, Jones advanced through local and sectional qualifying to make it to Oakland Hills. He gave himself a chance just by getting to the Open. As Sandy Tatum once said, "We want to identify the best player." The USGA provides a format, the players decide the outcome.

Tiger Woods has a chance to win at Pinehurst in 2005, and so does the last qualifier who makes the trip to the Sandhills region of North Carolina with a dream.

The Timeless Open

"Most players don't have the ability to hang in there, swallow your pride and hit shots [around the greens] that you don't normally hit. It tests your mental aspect, your mental approach, and it's a challenge," Woods said.

For so many people who witnessed the U.S. Open at Pinehurst in 1999—the event was staged on a golf course that is timeless—Phil Mickelson, Tiger Woods and Tim Herron were taking a little too much time. The USGA did not like the separation between their group and the rest of the field during the final two days. The USGA put each player on the clock for what they deemed was slow play on the final two days. Woods said, "It's tough being on the clock, because you look at these greens and when you miss them it's tough. You get some weird shots and it takes some time to figure them out, and you don't want to blow it, but you don't want to get a bad time. I got a bad time on 12 [Saturday], because the wind changed on me. If I was to get a one-shot penalty [for slow play] and miss winning the U.S. Open by one shot that would be pretty tough to swallow."

So many of the players argued that the pace of play rule needed an amendment, the Pinehurst No. 2 amendment, so that deliberate play was tolerated. "It takes time to figure out the slopes at Pinehurst. I understand there are exceptions to it. And, by looking at these greens, I think that's a pretty good exception," said Woods.

David Duval

Looking back at the 1999 U.S. Open, a lot of people don't remember a guy named Duval. David Duval showed up in Pinehurst with few expectations. A week before the

Open he suffered second-degree burns on his thumb and forefinger. Duval would have liked to tell the media that he burned his hand lighting the Olympic Cauldron at the opening ceremonies of the X-Games. But the steely-eyed wonder who had won four times on Tour in 1999 actually burned his hand on a teapot. His practice time was reduced to a single round before the Open, and on Friday night he was tied with Phil Mickelson and Payne Stewart for the lead. Duval was the No. 1-ranked player in the world at the time. He had won 11 times in less than three years, and he erased the early rise of Tiger Woods as the dominant guy who won the Green Jacket in 1997. And Duval's evaluation of the winner was emphatic. "It's very easy to make a five or six out here. So, there's no reason to panic. The guy who backs up the smallest amount is going to win," said Duval. Unfortunately for Duval, his third-round 75 was his undoing. A front-nine 40 left him three strokes off the lead on Sunday morning.

When the event rolls around in 2005, Duval may be able to get his game back to square. If he does, someone might want to ask him about the bunker shot on nine on Sunday. "I really didn't deserve that. But the game does not care."

Greatest Open Ever?

Will it be remembered as the greatest Open ever? Like so many moments in golf history, it will take time. And we know time tocks a beat slower at Pinehurst. As the players descend in 2005, the memories will all come rushing back. This is a new Open. New conditions. The field will be totally different. Sure, some of the same names might make their way back on the leader board, but no one will be able to erase the flamingo-stanced Payne Stewart on the 72nd green from memory.

It was at the home of golf. It was the last Open of the century. It was the last three holes. Before the 1999 Open began, Stewart tracked down his friend Tom Meeks of the USGA. Stewart said, "I've got a problem with 16." Meeks asked, "What's wrong with it?" The eventual champion said, "Why don't you just move the tee back and make it a par-five?"

Meeks said, "If I did that and you hit a big drive down there, are you going to go for the green, or are you going to lay up?

Stewart didn't hesitate. "I am going for the green."

Meeks tossed back, "You just answered my question." He added, "If you can get everybody in the field to sign a petition that says if we move the tee back, and we play it as a par-five, and nobody will go for the green in 2, then we'll play it as a par-five. But, of course nobody is going to do that."

It was Stewart who noted that week, "At Pinehurst, there is always the ability to run your ball up on the green." Ross would often send a warning to players who elected to dare play such a shot into his greens.

"There is little to be gained by those who elect to run the gauntlet of this opening," Ross said. And because of this, long-time president of Pinehurst Inc. and the USGA,

Richard Tufts, said, "Ross considered the ability to play the longer irons the supreme test of a great player." What Tufts and Ross didn't count on was the advent of technology, which has allowed the best amateur and professional players the ability to hit shorter irons into the greens at Pinehurst and other top courses around the world.

When the movie *Follow the Sun* came out in 1951, it recounted the horrific auto accident of Ben Hogan and chronicled his comeback. Typically such a movie is made when the protagonist is past his prime. But Hogan was just getting hot like the sun. He showed up at the Donald Ross-designed Oakland Hills after Robert Trent Jones had just renovated it. Hogan played the first two days conservatively, and 76-73 was the result. He had to treat his legs by soaking them at night so that he could walk the hilly layout just north of Detroit. He changed his tactics for round three and decided to attack the course. His 71 put him two strokes behind the pace set by Bobby Locke and Jimmy Demaret. In the afternoon round, he walked up to Ike Grainger, who served as the referee for the final round and said, "I'm going to burn it up." His outward nine was nothing special, even par 35, but the sun was getting hot on the back nine with birdies at 10, 13 and 15. Walking up to the 18th tee, he felt a par would win him the U.S. Open championship. He cleared the fairway bunkers with his drive and hit a 6-iron to 15 feet (the same distance Stewart had at Pinehurst). His birdie putt rolled dead center. U.S. Open Champion. "I'm glad that I brought this course, this monster, to its knees."

Hogan wasn't a long shot in 1951, he would have been considered a favorite, unlike in 1913, when two Brits sailed to America to bring the U.S. Open trophy back to their homeland. Harry Vardon and Ted Ray were the odds-on favorites to win the prized silver at the Country Club in Boston. Ouimet had never even qualified for the U.S. Amateur match-play portion of the event, let alone competed in the U.S. Open. Nonetheless, the single advantage he had over the other competitors was local knowledge. The three competitors were tied after three rounds. They really didn't need to play the fourth round, as each player posted a 79 (Ouimet needed to play the last six holes in two-under).

The 18-hole playoff was shocking. Ouimet, flanked by his 10-year-old caddie, Eddie Lowery, fired a 72 to beat Vardon and Ray. The gallery hoisted Ouimet on their shoulders and carried him around like a trophy.

In 1950 with Hogan and in 1964 with Ken Venturi, the last one standing was the U.S. Open Champion.

Hogan overcame his brutal car accident just 16 months prior to edge Lloyd Mangrum and George Fazio at Merio Golf Club, just outside of Philadelphia. As Hogan was faltering with bogeys on 12, 15 and 17, he fell back in a tie with Mangrum and Fazio. It was his 1-iron shot, one of the most famous shots in golf, to the final green, which allowed him to make par that capped the tournament. He won the U.S. Open in a playoff on Monday, shooting 69.

Venturi battled heat exhaustion and the recurring ailment of a pinched nerve he suffered in 1962. The 36-hole (double round) final day was played in heat near 100 degrees. Dr. John Everett and USGA executive director Joe Dey walked with Venturi for the final holes. Everett diagnosed Venturi with heat exhaustion before the final 18 and had administered salt tablets and tea. Tommy Jacobs faltered, and Venturi hung on for a four-stroke win, ending a four-year slump. The next year the USGA decided not to play the final two rounds on Saturday.

Then, of course, there is the 1982 Pebble Beach showdown between Tom Watson and Jack Nicklaus. If Sarazen's 4-wood at the 1935 Masters for double eagle was a shot heard 'round the world, and if Hogan's 1-iron at Merion at the 1950 Open was the clinching swing, then Watson's wedge from just off the par-three 17th in 1982 was definitely in the top 10. Watson told his caddie, Bruce Edwards, that he was going to make the shot just as if Babe Ruth pointed to the spot where his home run would land. Watson's shot hit the fringe and darted into the cup. He edged Nicklaus by one and then finished off the championship with another birdie at 18.

This is the context for what happened at Pinehurst in 1999. Payne Stewart had breakfast with his wife, Tracey, which included a few mangoes. He warmed up on Maniac Hill, where he ran into his old teacher, Harvie Ward. He had his caddie, Mike Hicks, retrieve a pair of scissors to turn his supplex wind jacket into a vest. With the tam o'shanter cap firmly in place, he eventually made it to the 16th hole where he faced the apex of the mountain in the final round of the century's last U.S. Open. Only four players reached what was called "Meeks's par four" on Sunday in regulation. Both Mickelson and Stewart faced the test of making four from off the green. Stewart's third was a miss-hit skidder that ended up 25 feet from the cup. The double-breaking putt was, as Mickleson later said, "the putt of a champion."

No matter where the 1999 U.S. Open ends up in the history of golf, one thing will remain constant. The U.S. Open is not a one-round tournament. And Pinehurst is not a one-hole golf course. Pinehurst golf is the sum of all its parts. It is arguably not the manicured brilliance of Augusta, or the seaside drama of Pebble Beach. Pinehurst is a sleeping giant where the sequencing of the first three holes leaves you guessing when there will be a reprieve. And in the end it is just as Donald Ross said at the beginning—a fair test of championship golf.

After all, the USGA doesn't want to demoralize the best players in the world, it wants to identify him.

One Symbol in Time

The difficulty of the "one moment in time" putt at Pinehurst and the tragic plane crash that ended Payne Stewart's life—they both seemed surreal.

How could the most important major at the end of the most incredible century of golf be followed by the death of the champion?

As PGA Tour players came to grips with the death of Stewart, the Scottish lament "Going Home" was played by Steve Agan. This was the only sound that could be heard in Houston at the Tour Championship.

Stewart was a friend to few until late in his career. One of his flock toward the end of his days was a young player named Bob Estes, who was coming of age. Estes decided, as he dealt with the grief of Stewart's death, that he would pay a personal tribute to the guy whom he had become extremely close to for the prior six months of Stewart's life.

Estes walked to the first tee of the Champion's Club to begin what was going to be an anguishing round to open the Tour Championship. After being announced, Estes teed up his ball very low, grabbed his putter from his bag and mumbled, "This is for Payne Stewart." His putt went about 15 feet, just as he planned. The same distance Stewart's putt traveled before finding the cup at the 72nd hole at Pinehurst. Brent Geiberger played next and knocked his tee shot down the fairway. Estes then knocked a 3-wood down the fairway and proceeded to make a double-bogey six on the hole.

Zinger

"It's really hard to grasp, really, that a tragedy of that magnitude could have happened to the current U.S. Open Champion," Paul Azinger said of Stewart's death.

"Payne needed that U.S. Open more than you did," Azinger said to Phil Mickelson at Stewart's funeral. "And now you know why. And it's funny, but I really—now more than ever—am a firm believer in whatever happens, happens for a reason."

Paul Azinger knows how to play golf at Pinehurst. He won the 1992 Tour Championship using a funny-looking teardrop-shaped putter he grabbed out of his neighbor's garage. When he won that year, his six-year-old daughter, Sarah Jean, was tugging at his leg when he said, "To win at Pinehurst is something special. I said the other day, it's the hardest course I've ever played."

Azinger's 12th place at the 1999 U.S. Open was non-descript, but he shared some secrets about the golf course with his friend Payne Stewart. After all, when he claimed the top prize in 1992, he shot 276 (eight under par). Stewart won the trophy in 1999 with a one-under-par score.

It was almost a year to the day that Payne Stewart teed off on the first hole at Pinehurst to claim the championship, and Azinger was organizing a ceremony held at the 2000 U.S. Open at Pebble Beach in which every player in the field was invited to hit a shot into the Pacific Ocean as a ceremonial tribute to Stewart.

"This is really golf's last opportunity to say good-bye to Payne. Even though it's only 30 minutes, I think we just need to honor the defending champion, and the man himself, one more time," said Azinger.

Zinger is the same guy who battled back from cancer. He is the same guy who was picked by Curtis Strange for the 2001 Ryder Cup team because of his heart and competitive spirit, and the same guy who had his best year on the golf course in 1993. Before Zinger was Zinger, he was a very average PGA Tour player. Heck, he didn't even break 40 until his senior year of high school. So starting on the PGA Tour was not something he needed to rush.

But what separates Zinger from the rest of the field at Pinehurst and anywhere else is that he knows the golf course. He knows the breaks in the greens, and he knows how to play low shots into the green so that the ball comes to rest in a playable area.

But people will say what Azinger has achieved in his work away from golf far exceeds what he has done on the PGA Tour.

Just prior to the ceremony, Azinger said, "I don't ever want to forget what happened to Payne. But time, I think, is always a healer. But it can also be a revealer. I think a lot of things have been revealed to me through this time of healing." And it was Stewart, just prior to his death who said, "That's one thing Paul [Azinger] taught me. Golf isn't everything."

Azinger first remembers Stewart showing up at the 1982 Magnolia Classic in Hattiesburg, Mississippi. This was the pre-tam o'shanter cap-and-knickers days. Azinger asked someone about the player with earrings. He said that they weren't earrings, they were acupuncture needles, and they were to help him concentrate. It turns out, the player with the acupuncture needles was the champion of the 1982 Magnolia Classic.

He adds, "I told Phil Mickelson that he should really understand the impact Payne's death had on the world. And that impact was magnified by the fact he was the United States Open Champion."

On June 14, 2000, at approximately 7:30 a.m., the PGA Tour and its players all said goodbye to Payne Stewart with the equivalent of a 21-gun salute as balls sailed into the Pacific Ocean.

The Statue

Tracey Stewart said, "Pinehurst was a special place to Payne, not only because he won his last U.S. Open Championship there, but also for the rich golf tradition that it represents." Stewart, her two children, Aaron and Chelsea,

USGA executive director David Fay, caddie Mike Hicks and Payne's long-time friend Paul Azinger all attended the unveiling of a life-size bronze statue of Stewart in November of 2001. The brief ceremony commemorated the champion's climactic putt on the 72nd hole and served as the third statue in Pinehurst's "Walk of Fame," adjacent to the 18th green. His likeness stands next to Donald Ross and Richard Tufts.

The ceremony included a bagpipe presentation by the St. Andrews Presbyterian College. Tracey Stewart and sculptor Zenos Frudakis were extremely adamant that Payne's foot be allowed to rest in the lawn of the garden. Frudakis, along with Hayter Fiurn, Pinehurst's landscape architectural firm, confirmed that the pose would accent the aesthetical qualities of this landmark spot at Pinehurst. The statue, which weighs 350 pounds, was originally formed in clay before it was sent to a Phildelphia-based casting company. It took Frudakis more than 18 months from the initial research to complete the statue. Several stances were suggested, but the animated pose was selected for the memorial. The one-legged fist pump commemorates the single moment Payne's putt nestled in the cup in the championship's final green.

It was suggested that the positioning of the statue appear to be in conversation with the statues of Tufts (also done by Frudakis) and Ross. Frudakis also did the statues of Arnold Palmer and Bobby Jones at Augusta National.

And the words "One Moment in Time" are engraved at the base of the statue. Paul Azinger said, "Payne's putt is *the* defining moment of his career."

One Logo in Time

Less than two months after the "One Moment in Time" statue was introduced, came the reminder of a renewed sense of purpose at Pinehurst. The introduction of the 2005 U.S. Open logo, created by Stephen Cryan, the director of merchandising at Pinehurst and the artistic talents of Susan Wiedenmeyer, a freelance artist based in Lenexa, Kansas.

The championship's return to Pinehurst is the quickest turnaround in the championship's history since it was contested at Inverness in 1940 and 1946. USGA executive director Mike Butz said, "The '99 Open was arguably the most successful and exciting Open Championship we have achieved in recent history. On 2005 we look forward to adding another chapter of history on famed No. 2."

The logo once again features the Golf Lad, who originally was introduced in advertising in 1909. He will be featured in a white floppy hat, khaki pants and a red shirt. He is swinging a short iron with a modern-day shaft. An American flag was added to the background of the logo to give it the traditional patriotic impression.

This statue, located near the 18th green, serves as a remembrance of the 1999 U.S. Open Champion—Payne Stewart.

Donald Ross.

4

Donald Ross

Tracing the past of Donald Ross leads one to the tiny town of Dornoch, Scotland. Born in 1872, Ross grew up in this coastal area "keeping the green" at the Dornoch Golf Club. He also became adept at club making and playing the game.

As a young man, he left for one year to become an apprentice at St. Andrews under Od Tom Morris. It was Morris who laid out the first nine holes at Dornoch.

In the mid-1980s when Tom Watson was being courted by Britain for his brilliant play in the Open, he would find time before or after the championship to head to the Royal Dornoch Golf Club. In 1981, just after he won his third of five British Open titles, he headed north to play Royal Dornoch. He ended up playing three rounds, saying it was the most fun he had ever had on a golf course.

Former club captain at Dornoch, John Macleod wrote *A History of the Royal Dornoch Golf Club* and reported: "The first three golf links in Scotland of which there is written record are: St. Andrews (1552), Leith (1593) and Dornoch (1616)."

In 1616, Morris had finished the nine holes, and three years later nine more were added. Macleod writes, "About the turn of the century the great Sandy Herd played with the new rubber-cored ball and out of fashion went the old gutty. John Sutherland, who guided Dornoch as the club secretary for over 50 years, and his committee had to remodel the course as a result of the faster ball, and Dornoch became for a time the fifth longest course in Britain."

It is understood that because Ross spent so much time examining the contour and layout of the early Dornoch that he took a lot of his understanding of golf from the course. Even though Ross eventually was involved with the design of more than 400 courses in the United States, Dornoch was the original links design where he learned to play and also came to understand the fair and penal aspects of the game.

And it was at Pinehurst that he implemented the grasses and turf management strategies that revolutionized how America would come to understand the game of golf. This wasn't completely realized until he converted the oiled sand greens to Bermuda grass prior to hosting the 1935 PGA Championship.

Golf historian and writer Bradley S. Klein writes, "Of all the courses that bear Ross's name, either as original designs or as renovation projects, he probably never saw a third of them, and another third he visited only once or twice. Given the constraints of train and car travel in those days, repeat visits were difficult to arrange. Though Ross was a vicarious traveler, he did much of his design work from his home in a cottage behind the third green at Pinehurst. There he worked from topographic maps, drew up blueprints, and wrote simple, but sharply worded instructions that his construction crew knew how to implement."

Looking at the course description of Dornoch, it is easy to see how he blended his appreciation for great layouts to his American designs. The second hole at Dornoch is a 177-yard par three. It's described as: "A plateau green [one of many] with steep falls on both sides and rear. Two deep bunkers guard the front of the green, with a grassy mound between, which diverts short shots into either bunker." Harvie Ward has played Royal Dornoch several times. He said, "My friend lives on the second hole. And the only difference between No. 2 and Royal Dornoch is that we have trees."

It could be said that Ross brought the same kind of opening shots to America, but created dastardly greens complex with bunkers, swales and tight grass that reward great shots and leave marginal shots with options, usually none of them very appealing.

Innes Dornoch and Out

Donald Ross was not the only resident of Dornoch, Scotland who descended on Pinehurst and made it his life-long home. Rod Innes, born in Dornoch in 1911, moved with his family to Pinehurst in 1922.

While in Dornoch, Innes came to know the Ross family well. Innes said, "He was a very precise individual. In my hometown [Dornoch], he belonged to the Free Church of Scotland. It was the original Presbyterian Church. And it was one of those churches where they had no artificial music like an organ or a piano. The hymns would stand out because there was a person that would sing the line, and then the congregation would sing the line. And that is what Donald would do—he would sing a line and the congregation would repeat it. That church still stands today."

Innes said, "Donald was chosen to learn something about golf, so the people at Dornoch subsidized him to learn from Tom Morris, and I think he also got an education in St. Andrews from club making from the shops along the Firth. While he was at Dornoch he was also apprenticed by a man named Peter Murray."

Ross gravitated to Pinehurst after time in New England at around the turn of the century. Innes moved to Pinehurst in 1922, and got a job in Ross's golf shop. By this time, Ross had built quite a reputation for his early architectural work. Innes remembers his exactness in making sure the games equipment (hickory shafts) were fit for play. "People would bring in broken shafts, and we would replace them. There were all kinds—MacGregor, Spaulding. Ross sure knew how to make a club from the ground up," Innes said.

Innes will never forget the day Ross came behind the counter in the golf workshop. "There were three of us working on the bench, and he looked behind me and saw a chisel. It was an old chisel that I didn't give a hoot about. I was using it to take the tacks out of the shaft. In those days we used to tack the grips to the shaft." Ross grabbed the chisel and went into the backroom and asked one of the workers to turn the wheel on the grinder. Ross put a beautiful finish on the chisel and glared at Innes. Ross said, "I don't ever want to come back here and see tools like that lying around." Innes scoffed, "He didn't realize that that tool was making him money." He adds, "He was a precise fellow, indeed."

Innes recalls the days when the steel shafts and the True Temper Co. were slowly replacing the hickory shafts. Innes said, "It was long about 1929 and they came out with the steel shaft. Some changed, and the old timers stayed with the old hickory. We would use an adapter to change the shafts, it really did not work very well."

The other part of the game that was changing rapidly was the golf ball. Innes said, "We used the old gutta-balls. And Bobby Jones came up to play Pinehurst on a March day in the early '30s. It was a very windy day and everybody noticed that the ball Jones was using was going past everyone else's," said Innes. What happened next is a timeless story in golf. "We all found out that Jones was using one of those paintless Spaulding balls and the cover was complete— it was balata. Anyway, we looked at the ball, and the golf shop just happened to have a gross of them. They sold in nothing flat." Innes was witness to the game's ever-changing pace in the 1930s. The sand greens became grass, the club shafts became steel and the ball was continuing to evolve.

And while the game's equipment was switching gears, Innes saw Ross from the inside. He was friends with his daughter, Lillian, and shortly after Ross's wife passed away, he had pictures of Ross as he returned to Dornoch. He also found Ross's personality to be exacting, and he also saw him to be exhaustingly hard working. The architectural process Ross used with his chief engineer in Rhode Island, W. Irving Johnson, intrigued Innes. "Ross would get a topographical map from a course he was designing to determine elevation change and things. Then he would outline where he wanted the holes to be. With an individual pen he would add a sketch of what the individual hole would look like, whether it was a straightaway or dogleg. The process was really clever," said Innes. He adds, "Ross only had an eighth or ninth grade education, but he was really clever."

When Innes and his family first moved to Pinehurst, he estimated the total town to be comprised of between 900 and 1,000 people mostly from New England, Ohio and Pennsylvania. A lot of the families came down and built cottages on Linden Road. At first, the resort operated on a seasonal basis. Innes remembers, "The Holly Inn had the same clientele year after year until they died. Everything at the [Holly] was top grade. They printed a separate menu for every meal."

Many of the old wealthy families, including the Eberhart-Fabers (yes, the pencils) dissipated. Innes gravitated to banking in Pinehurst. And in later years he invested in the Primrose Cottage, once owned by Ross.

Innes fondly recalls the days when life in Pinehurst was simple.

"To some, the only thing Pinehurst offered was golf."

St. Andrews vs. Pinehurst

It is really very simple. St. Andrews is the home of golf. Pinehurst is the home of golf in America; some 19th holers think this is open for debate. Others consider what happened at Brookline in the late 19th century and the Ouimet Open (1913) and want to fuel the argument. The California crowd adds Pebble Beach as the home of golf in America.

St. Andrews is the home of golf. There is no other place so rich in heritage and hallowed in its raw architecture of the land. One of the first references of the game came from the diary of a student in 1574. James Melville wrote that his father provided him with "glub an' bals fur goff but nocht a purss fur catch pull and tavern." This translates into "club and balls for golf but nothing for hand tennis or drinking in the pub," as written in the *History of St. Andrews* by David Joy.

The road hole, the Swilken Bridge, and the barren land with all of its subtle contours remind anyone who arrives in Scotland that this is the way golf is supposed to be played.

Back in America is Pinehurst No. 2, the village, and a portrait by Norman Rockwell on how life on Main Street remains timeless.

Could the game in America be any more mundane than at Pinehurst? Unconventional and unnatural obstacles like water hazards, narrow, tree-lined fairways and greenside stadium contours allow for maximum gallery viewing. This course is naked. The land gives way to the golf course. The golf course does not demand space but enjoys it, a certain co-existence with the natural surroundings, just like at St. Andrews. At the 1999 U.S. Open, Nick Price said it best: "It is really a shame that television is not three dimensional, so the folks watching at home could see how severe all these humps and bumps are around the edges of the greens."

In 1900, the *Pinehurst Outlook* reported, "Throughout the winter the climate of Pinehurst is especially favorable for the enjoyment of golf, the clear blue sky and bright warm sunshine tempting old and young, weak and strong, to indulge in this healthful game. Golf was undoubtedly the most popular pastime in the village last year." In 1902, the No. 2 course was opened. More than a century later and not much has changed.

The Way Ross Would Have Wanted It

"They have maintained the integrity of Donald Ross and the way you should play it. This is an international Open," said Greg Norman on the eve of the 1999 U.S. Open.

Norman was outspoken on the understated test of a challenging layout. "He built this as a second-shot golf course by the way he built the greens. There's not a lot of trouble off the tees. And the way these greens are built, they're inverted, there exists a lot of runoff with that. The fifth hole is probably an 8,000-square-foot green, but it only has 700 square feet of pinnable surface. It's a very precise second-shot golf course, and that's the way Ross did it. That's the way Ross would have wanted it."

Building the Greens

Pinehurst No. 2 played like a parking lot in the 1970s. The greens were like rocks according to the premier player in the game, Jack Nicklaus. Pine needles and hard sandy soil was the only thing between the fairway and the trees. There was no rough. Not anymore.

Current greens superintendent Paul Jett came aboard in 1995 to prepare the course for its first U.S. Open. The USGA met with Jett and discussed the alterations needed to make the current game part of the old playground. He was interested in making the playground playable. Jett knows that Donald Ross did not have the irrigation system and he knows that the game the Scots brought to America was not as much about the playground. That has changed. Now, the USGA and the Open venue team up years in advance to get it right. They discuss the widths of the fairways, the slopes in the greens and the elevation of tee boxes. Much of the decision to bring the U.S. Open to Pinehurst in 1999 was predicated on the agreement that the No. 2 greens be rebuilt. It happened in 1996. "It was a two-month process in terms of the time we put a hole in the ground to the time we added the seed," said Jett. He adds, "Despite the need to cover the greens from two hurricanes, it went smooth from start to finish."

Pinehurst No. 2 has been tinkered with over the years. The greens were re-surfaced in 1987, prior to the 1990 and 1991 PGA Tour Championships. And the game has changed with the technology of turf-grass equipment. And the next time the Open comes to town, the wet conditions of the

1999 U.S. Open may be long forgotten. "The course will likely play a lot different, depending on the weather," said Jett.

The Wiregrass and the Love Grass

As Donald Ross developed the Sandhills region for golf, he encountered grasses that he was not familiar with, coming from Dornoch, Scotland. One of these was a peculiar gray-green grass that became part of his legacy at Pinehurst. Introducing the plant known by some naturalists as the "botanical believe it or not"—wiregrass. Some know it as *Atrida stricata,* which sounds like a classical song. Its generic name, wiregrass, makes it a presence from Carolina pine forests all the way to Mississippi. It derives its name from the wire-like leaves that spring out like tentacles. To some naturalists, the plant was vital to the ecosystem, because it is resistant to drought and for years has served as sort of kindling for pine forests. Naturalist B.W. Wells said, "It is a lot like stretched out toothpicks and it serves as a pile of the finest slivered kindling wood." This helped spread fires, which helped the pine forests survive by not being overrun by wood tree species that would eventually replace the pines. The golfers at Pinehurst see both wiregrass and its imported brethren, love grass, as a nuisance to a good golf score.

The strange thing about wiregrass is that it remains standing for several years even after it dies. And like Ross's legacy, the natural terrain he carved, including the wiregrass, lives on.

It can be argued that the grasses add to the penal aspect of golf at Pinehurst.

Golf course superintendent Paul Jett said, "The wiregrass is "native to this part of the country, whereas the love grass was imported." He adds, "You see pictures of Donald Ross standing out in what was supposed to be a fairway. Up until the mid-1970s, that is what the rough at Pinehurst really was—Bermuda grass fairways, then it would give way into rough, waste area, sand and wiregrass."

The No. 2 course has four holes that have dedicated wiregrass areas, 3, 8, 11 and 12. "It provides another penalty to the player should they land in an area where there is wiregrass and love grass," said Jett.

Jett is not so sure where the love grass got its name, but he knows that its growth pattern has made its long-term existence at Pinehurst one of the ticking clocks of the resort. He said, "The love grass will grow so fast, so tall and so thick, that if someone hits their ball in it, there is a chance you are not going to find it."

These two grasses are really indicative of what Ross tried to accomplish: Use the natural terrain of the region and make it part of the game's challenge.

Par Reduction

The No. 2 course yardage book calls the 489-yard 16th a "par five for resort play." That's kind of like saying mere mortals play the monster-yardage hole to five strokes, but since you have a PGA Tour card, we will give you four strokes, raised rough and the wind is your problem. The 16th hole factored into only 11 birdies during the four days of play in the 1999 U.S. Open. The stroke average was 4.5 strokes— advantage to the hole. The 16th figured as the second most difficult hole in the championship. The par-four fifth was the most difficult at 4.55 strokes for the defining level players.

In the *mano e mano* battle between Mickelson and Stewart, the 16th made a difference. Both players managed to miss the green with their approach shots. Stewart, short and left, pitched his shot past the hole, leaving himself a 20-foot downhill putt for par. Mickleson showed his talent around the shaven greens, leaving himself a six-footer. At one under, Mickelson had the clear advantage to pad his lead.

Not so fast. Stewart drained his putt to transfer the heat to Mickelson. The lefty pulled his putt. "The tendency for me, and it wasn't just Sunday, but all week, was to pull my putts a little. I read that putt as a double breaker and I just pulled it a little too far right to get all the way back to the left," said Mickelson.

Stewart saw the 16th as the turning point. "For some reason I felt like I needed to make a move then. I ending up charging my chip, but it ended up all working out."

Although the final two shared the spotlight at Pinehurst, don't forget the rest of the field had to play the hole. Vijay Singh did not sing the praises of the hole after he was even par going into 70th hole of the championship. A drive into the deep left rough, a second shot that headed low and left, again in the rough, a wedge past the hole and two putts sent the defending PGA Champion to one-over par. He would not recover.

The lone player among the leaders to beat the 16th was Tiger Woods. A 3-iron approach shot to within 12 feet of the cup led to a fist pump. Unfortunately for Woods, the par-three 17th was his undoing. A bogey cost him a chance at the prize and led to a final-round 70 and a tie with Singh.

The 16th is as challenging a par four as there is in major championship golf. It will certainly be on the players' minds as they prepare for the 2005 U.S. Open.

If Not Now, When?

If Pinehurst is the heart of American golf, then why did it take the USGA a century to find the tiny village for a major championship like the Open?

The answers are much like the Pinehurst greens—a little perplexing. And the excuses are a little like the rising fog on No. 2. The USGA rhetoric went something like this: *timing, temperature, turf grass and Tufts.*

The beginning of the non-invitation has to do with the status of the resort in the 1970s, a great decade for the *green* team on the baseball diamond in Oakland, but it was a tough decade for Pinehurst. The fairways were not green, they were biscuit brown. The sale of Pinehurst to Diamondhead caused the focus to stray from the fairways and greens and zero in on real estate sales.

At this time, the No. 2 course was a regular stop on the PGA Tour, but it was Thanksgiving for most players in terms of scoring and the time of the year. The phrase "fairways like air strips" was a prevailing theme. Tom Watson was a relatively new player on the PGA Tour in 1973. When he arrived in Pinehurst for the World Open, he certainly was not one of the favorites. An atypical PGA event, the World Open was like a golf marathon. It lasted two weeks and consisted of 144 holes. Prior to the 1973 event, the course record on the No. 2 layout was a pair of 65s by Ben Hogan and Johnny Palmer. The chilly November weather was somewhere north, and the first day allowed Gibby Gilbert to shoot a nine-under-par 62. Gilbert called the eight birdies, one eagle and one bogey round a "freak round."

Watson matched Gilbert's round two days later. Then, in 1977, Hale Irwin fired another 62 to finish 20 under par. Enough was enough.

By 1980, the course regained its footing and began to host the end of the season Tour Championship. Scheduling in the early fall proved to provide relief to the burnt-out Bermuda. This was the start of a second look for Pinehurst. The reviews when Craig Stadler and Paul Azinger won in 1981 and 1982 proved to be little louder than a mild gallery golf clap.

The grass was beginning to be evaluated and the restoration of the golf course would hit a different gear in 1984 when Club Corp. bailed out Diamondhead of its holdings. A rebirth of golf began to take shape and the lure of a major championship was not as integral as restoring the golf heritage.

And Pinehurst had a rich history in amateur golf. Richard Tufts made sure that the hallmark of Pinehurst golf was firmly planted on the game as it was intended at the beginning of the century. The only problem was that the game was changing to include more entertainment. The movie *Caddyshack* helped spark this, and the PGA Tour was becoming recognized as a viable weekend option. Tufts, the man who sculpted the growth, was a USGA insider. His close association with Pinehurst kept the U.S. Amateur away for more years than Billy Joe Patton could endure. And any favoritism toward the recruitment of the game on any level was, of course, a conflict of interest. Why travel down the cart path of favoritism when the game of golf was built on being humble? Humility and anonymity somehow pervaded. At Pinehurst, amateur golf was king.

And Pinehurst is not exactly a major metropolitan setting. The USGA has avoided backwoods venues for the obvious: lodging, travel and convenience. A major hurdle was the 1972 U.S. Open at Pebble Beach. A remote resort location that is not readily accessible, it passed the test.

Pinehurst handled the lodging, the corporate handshakes, the traffic, the concessions, and a divine power handled the weather. The most impressive statistic had to do with the contributions of the Pinehurst volunteers. In such a small town, how did so many people arrive to pitch in?

Pinehurst passed the test in 1999 and the quick return for 2005 has a lot to do with one *major* factor: the golf course.

Fore—No. 4

So much has been made of Pinehurst No. 2 that some of the other Pinehurst courses, if personified, might blush at the adjectives thrown in its direction. If Pinehurst is the home of golf, the No. 2 course was the foundation.

In the mid-1990s, Tom Fazio, arguably the best contemporary designer in the game, was asked to examine Pinehurst No. 4. In the opinion of the Pinehurst front office he was told to do what he had to do to turn it into a championship layout. At the time, No. 4 was a bit of a discard.

Donald Ross did the original design of No. 4, (1914) and over the last 50 years it was tweaked by notables Robert Trent Jones Sr. (1973) and Rees Jones (1983) before it landed on the drafting board of a man in the Western Carolina mountains—Fazio.

Fazio looked at several options to upgrade the course. It served as a parking lot, housed corporate tents and other ancillary holdings for the 1999 U.S. Open. During the week of the Open Championship, Davis Love III remarked, "I spent a lot of time on No. 4, it is kind of tough to see it as a parking lot." Its opening shortly after Stewart's triumph in 1999 signaled a new beginning for the course that many felt was outdated.

As a tribute to Ross and as a punctuation mark on his genius, Fazio did more by doing a little. He kept a majority of the same hole routing that Ross used, but added waste bunkers such as those on holes seven and 18. He used the contour of the land to position false fronts on some greens and added some inverted saucer mounds in greens to repel the poorly played approach—a Ross stamp. He added bunkers, and their placement spells trouble from tee to green. It became more of a complete course.

"It is a wonderful layout, and as a modern-day layout, it is outstanding," said Ken Crow, who has worked with the Pinehurst golf circles for the past 20 years. Crow insists that if there was a way to begin to explore golf at Pinehurst, No. 4 would be the perfect starting point.

Until Fazio got his hands on the first couple of holes and began placing a myriad of bunkers, No. 4 was just another course at Pinehurst.

Insiders now know that No. 4 is the real deal. From caddies to the director of golf, Matt Massei, people who show up at Pinehurst get an earful on No. 4.

"Mr. Fazio did an outstanding job. His vision was remarkable. No. 4 has its own identity, but it fits in with the family," said Massei.

A better testimony to how No. 4 stacks up was recently issued by the USGA. They will play two qualifying rounds of stroke play on the course for the 2007 U.S. Amateur.

The votes are rolling in, and the balls are rolling off the green at No. 4. Soon to be tabbed one of the best new "modern" courses in the country.

It is moving up the ladder.

5

Two Diverging Paths

The North and South Open was discontinued in 1951, just as the PGA Tour was gaining speed. At this time, the PGA Tour was abandoning the practice of free room and board to professionals. They would then add the equivalent value of this sum to the purses. As written in the *Pinehurst Outlook*, "It became quite clear that present-day professional golf had nothing to contribute to the development of a true golfing atmosphere at Pinehurst."

The hope of James W. Tufts when Pinehurst was founded was "to establish a small, friendly community where those in need of relaxation, either for years of their retirement or for the purpose of equipping them to perform their daily tasks more efficiently…Golf came to America as the great amateur sport, rich with tradition and enjoying the highest possible standards of ethics and good sportsmanship in its play. The idea has been to accept the game at Pinehurst in this form and to maintain and preserve these standards in order that amateur golfers may find at Pinehurst those things which James Tufts sought to provide."

The year 1951 was a turning point for golf in America and for the North and South Open. "I really don't think Dick Tufts was too pleased with the reaction of some of the top players in the game. It was his decision to discontinue play," said long-time amateur Bill Campbell.

With the 1951 Ryder Cup in November, the North and South Open took a backseat. Some feel it never recovered. The 1951 Ryder Cup was an event that marked a change in the game and a change in Pinehurst.

1951 Ryder Cup

"He got down with a splash and a putt 10 times," said Great Britain's Dai Rees of Jimmy Demaret's ability to get up and down from the sand in their singles match.

"They could not get accustomed to the Bermuda grass or play with your larger ball with real expertness," captain Arthur Lacey said of his team's Ryder Cup loss in 1951.

In 1927, Samuel Ryder presented the Ryder Cup to Great Britain's Professional Golfers Association. The 17-inch trophy was valued at 250 pounds. Today, the cup is worth an estimated $13,900. The Golfer depicted on the top of the trophy is Abe Mitchell, friend and private instructor of Ryder.

In 1951, the Ryder Cup was contested at Pinehurst. The then two-day event (fourball was not introduced until 1963) was suspended on Saturday so that both teams could attend the North Carolina vs. Tennessee football game in Chapel Hill. Tennessee won the game, 27-0. The time-out for football did not re-energize the European squad that was down three to one entering Sunday's singles matches. All singles matches before 1961 were 36-hole matches. The U.S. won or halved seven of the eight singles matches on Sunday on their way to a $9^1/_2$ to $2^1/_2$ win. Dai Rees, the venerable Brit who would eventually finish his career in 1961 after nine appearances, was mesmerized in his match with American Jimmy Demaret. Demaret found 11 greenside bunkers. Demaret capped his match by holing out from the greenside bunker on the 17th hole to win two-up. After the match he handed his sand wedge to Rees as a gift. Rees was so taken by the club that he had an identical one made for his bag.

The year's U.S. Open champion, Ben Hogan, found himself down two holes after six holes against the veteran internationalist, Charles Ward. He wound up beating Ward 3 and 2 with some unbelievable play in the afternoon. He started his second 18 with a birdie on the first two holes. And on the eighth hole he made an eagle three on the 488-yard hole after he hit a large brassie to the edge of the green. Ward came back with a two on the par-three ninth. But Hogan won the 10th, 15th and 16th as Ward failed to win another hole. Match over.

But the hero of the matches was likely Stewart "Skip" Alexander. Alexander was a victim of an airplane crash in Evansville, Indiana in 1950. Alexander, a one-time captain of the Duke golf team was not sure whether he would be able to grip the club in the cold Carolina conditions. The matches were contested on November 3 and 5, not like the September timetable that exists for the current Ryder Cup matches.

His win was the most lopsided of the Ryder Cup. He beat John Panton 8 and 7. The *Pinehurst Outlook* account said: "And you should have seen cute Mr. Alexander's smile when he and Jack Panton shook hands as the cameras clicked."

Sam Snead, the captain for the U.S. effort, also led the charge on the course. He teamed with Lloyd Magrum for a 5 and 4 win on foursomes and beat Max Faulkner 4 and 3 in singles to anchor the win.

The triumph was the Americans' seventh Cup in nine tries since the matches began.

Great Britain's captain, Arthur Lacey, summed up the losing effort. "I don't want to make any excuses as I congratulate a fine, winning team. But our boys did not play from bunkers well nor were their short approaches as accurate as the Americans."

The 1951 Ryder Cup was a turning point in the history of American golf. Richard Tufts was at the eye of the storm. Soon after the Ryder Cup in 1951, the North and South Open would be played at Pinehurst. There was little interest from the American team to play in the event. Tufts was steaming and the event would be discontinued. The event, which had been a part of the success story for Pinehurst's early days of championship history, was wiped away.

Tufts turned his efforts to the rules of golf. In this same year, the stymie rule was discontinued. A collective sigh of relief was heard from New England to San Francisco. This outdated rule was "getting in the way" of the game's progress.

As the year came to a close, Ben Hogan had gone on a tear. Winning the U.S. Open in June at Oakland Hills, taming "the Monster," after claiming the Masters over Sam Snead. A little more than a decade earlier, Hogan was searching for his first win at Pinehurst.

Where's Jack?

Richard Tufts has been called one of the most ethical, understated men ever. He really did not want to campaign for Pinehurst, his family company, to host the U.S. Amateur. He did not want his personal affiliation to become an issue in hosting the event. Not that he thought Pinehurst would not be a great test. It was just too close to amateur golf nepotism that he fundamentally disagreed with.

Bill Campbell remembers being part of a group of players who showed up for the 1960 U.S. Amateur in St. Louis at the St. Louis Country Club. The course was ravaged by poor conditions.

"It certainly wasn't the fault of anyone, it just was not a great test of golf," remembers Campbell.

It was shortly after this event that a group of players started a petition to bring the Amateur to Pinehurst in 1962. The players decided to sign a petition and get it to the desk of Tufts.

Billy Joe Patton remembers, "It was more of a groundswell of people who had played there that thought it would reward what he considered the fairest test of golf."

The USGA, headed by Tufts, relented. The U.S. Amateur came to Pinehurst in 1962.

The field was packed with players and stories: Only the defending champion did not make the trip to Pinehurst. The 1961 U.S. Amateur Champion, Jack Nicklaus, turned professional, missing his chance to defend the title he nailed down with an 8 and 6 win over Dudley Wysong at Pebble Beach.

And so the field was wide open. Some of the favorites included Homero Blancas who had won the NCAA Championship for Houston. A 24-year-old Deane Beman, the 1960 U.S. Amateur Champion, Harvie Ward, winner of the North and South (1948), and U.S. Amateur Champion (1955-56) Billy Joe Patton were players in the field that many considered to be central to the outcome.

The press release for the championship was intriguing:

"The No. 2 layout is championship in every respect, and has been the scene of innumerable competitions, including the 1936 PGA, the Ryder Cup matches [1951], not to speak of the North and South Amateurs and Opens.

"If they survive the first seven matches of the rugged competition, they will play the final 36-hole match before the appreciative eyes of a golfer of no small fame himself, former president Dwight D. Eisenhower."

Junior Nothing

One junior playing in the field for the 1962 U.S. Amateur was anything but a junior. Charles Evans Jr., age 72, competed in his 50th consecutive U.S. Amateur. He won the tournament in 1916 and 1920. Evans won the Western Amateur eight times and played on three Walker Cup teams.

SMU Connection

There was a two-person connection to Southern Methodist University at the 1999 U.S. Open. No, not Eric Dickerson and Craig James. One graduated from the Business School in 1979, and the other one funded the Business School. Both were champions, and both are no longer with us. Payne Stewart, the most famous SMU golfer is one obvious choice, the other worked behind the scenes—Robert H. Dedman Sr., the self-proclaimed King of Clubs.

When he died in 2002, Dedman had more than 250 country clubs corralled under the name Club Corp. The reason for that approximate number is that Dedman was collecting more clubs by the New York minute up until his death on August 20, 2000.

It all started in 1957 when Dedman purchased 400 acres near Dallas. If it sounds familiar, this was nearly the same amount James W. Tufts purchased in central North Carolina in 1895. Dedman set out to develop Brookhaven Country Club.

His company was founded on a premise that the club could be a profitable business from the inside out. Names like Firestone Country Club (Akron, OH), Indian Wells (Indian Wells, CA) and Mission Hills (Rancho Mirage, CA) were all Club Corp. properties.

Pinehurst may be his grandest accomplishment. And not just because he turned things inside out on the business side of the resort. It wasn't until Dedman directed Pinehurst that the course was restored to the way Ross had intended it to be played. This all started in 1984 when he purchased Pinehurst from a consortium of banks. There were green jigsaw pieces all over. Dedman liked to think he was the king of putting the pieces of the puzzle together.

He earned an alphabet soup of undergraduate degrees from the University of Texas at Austin. He earned his Master's of Law Degree from SMU.

He often reflected that "We're in the business of selling fun." He liked to sell his ideas with phrases like "win-win," and he saw the game of golf through different lenses. "You don't have to be a golfer to understand that the game involves keeping score, hoping to win and learning to lose."

Dedman shot his age on the golf course (which he called his "playground") when he was 65.

Jack Nicklaus, who signed an agreement to build courses for Dedman in 1998, agrees his legacy will live on.

"He was the leader in how to make golf work as a business. What he created and built will serve as a model for many others in the industry for years to come."

The golf industry has lost two Mustangs—the Henry Ford of golf course management and the fun-loving champion's champion, Payne Stewart.

Campbell's Soul

"I once said that Pinehurst was a state of mind. What I really meant was that Pinehurst was a state of mind and heart," said Bill Campbell, former USGA president and long-time amateur stalwart.

Bill Campbell knows golf, and he is not afraid to wax eloquent about the place where he often found golfer's solace.

"At Pinehurst I feel the essence of the game. I feel the air wafting through the pines..."

Campbell would sometimes escape the village of Pinehurst noise by grabbing a book and sauntering behind the community chapel for a good read.

Campbell might be the second most recognizable figure in golf when he dons the tam o'shanter cap. He just received the Donald Ross award by the Donald Ross Society, awarded at Oakmont Country Club.

His record on the links is a long-running landslide. "I had my share of successes at Pinehurst in terms of winning and losing. He adds, "In 1952, I didn't head to Pinehurst because I was running for congress."

Campbell knows the heritage of Pinehurst. The Dornoch roots of Ross are well documented. During his acceptance speech at Oakmont, Campbell paraphrased a quote from a well-documented Scottish clergyman named

Jim Simpson of Dornoch Cathedral, explaining the differences in the game in America and the one abroad.

Twisting his dialect, Campbell started: "Americans seem to think that a good drive should land in the fairway and stay there. This permits an even lie, with an approach shot to an acceptable green and a makeable putt. We Scots know better. We know that drives sometimes come to rest in the rough. We know that bad bounces are part of the game. From a bad lie can come an even worse break. But we can make a recovery from a bad space…and thus, we always have a chance at redemption."

The one awe-inspiring aspect of Bill Campbell is that he is no different than Pinehurst personified. He understands his roots. He still lives in Huntington, WV. He knows his ability to play golf was a gift from a greater power.

He also has witnessed the resurgence of the land he knows as the home of American golf. He saw the resort slip out of the hands of Dick Tufts reluctantly. "They were conservative. If you had New England taste, you enjoyed what they did." He adds, "Diamondhead came in, and they were putting pine cones as ground-under repair."

Campbell watched as the resort went from 1,100 employees to 600 employees.

Bill Campbell picked up where Tufts left off in shaping the rules of golf. He has overseen the change of the Europeans' 1.62 ball to the Americans' 1.68 ball we recognize in play today. He was the USGA president when Forest Fizzler scampered into a port-a-john at the 1977 U.S. Open, changing into a pair of shorts. Prior to that he served as a quintessential amateur player. He won the U.S. Amateur in 1964 at Canterbury Golf Club in Cleveland. In the round of 16 he met and defeated his North Carolina friend, Billy Joe Patton. Prior to Campbell claiming the prize (the Havemayer Trophy), Deane Beman and a guy named Nicklaus claimed the cup four of the previous five years. Oh, and a guy named Harris won it in 1962 (See Summer of '62).

He first came to Pinehurst in 1942 as a member of the OCS 100th Infantry Division. He said, "It was a fairyland to me."

6

Changing Places

The 1970s were a time of change, especially at Pinehurst. Operated as a resort by the Tufts family, it was wilting and reeling with little direction. In December of 1970, the sale of five golf courses, clubhouse, various recreational facilities and more than 7,000 acres of undeveloped land was made to the Diamondhead Corporation, headed by Malcolm McLean.

In 1971, Pinehurst Inc. became the wholly owned subsidiary of Diamondhead. "The Tufts made an honest effort to run the place in the Tufts tradition," said Bill Campbell. He adds, "Dick Tufts did not want to sell the place. But he did not have majority control. They just ran out of green."

Pinehurst's initial vision included the re-birth of Pinehurst's real estate endeavors. House, condominium and land sales were aggressive. The World Golf Hall of Fame was developed; the Carolina Hotel went under a refurbishing and was renamed the Pinehurst Hotel. The village of Pinehurst was placed on the National Register of Historic Places. During the whirlwind to sell real estate and forge ahead, the Holly Inn was in decline. A decision was made to close the hotel rather than make needed renovations.

The golf course began to take a turn in the direction they thought would return it to a Scottish links course. The waste areas and bunkers started to grow "love grass." "Those were the days of getting a bad break in the bunker and being behind a clump of love grass," said longtime caddie Jeff Ferguson. Ferguson watched balls roll off the fairway and roll and roll and roll. "It was definitely a different style course than it is today," he added.

By the end of the decade there was a controversy swirling between the owner of Pinehurst and the village residents, which limited Club members' use of certain facilities.

By 1978, the financial problems escalated. There was a sea of red ink on the green-clad resort. More than $138 million was owed in short-term notes to a consortium of eight banks. The consortium began initially by divesting itself with a series of property settlements including property in the village. This is when Club Corporation of America stepped in and paid a reported $15 million for the holdings, which included six golf courses, three golf clubhouses, the tennis club, health spa, gun club and marina. One of the first steps was to build Course No. 7.

Club Corp. has worked closely with the village officials to restore Pinehurst to its proper place as a stately southern resort with all of its trimmings.

The idea was to turn Pinehurst into the "St. Andrews of America." Club Corp. started by paying attention to the most important playground—Pinehurst No. 2. The greens on Pinehurst No. 2 were revamped in 1987, a transformation that soon would bring the Tour Championship, the Senior U.S. Open and eventually two U.S. Opens.

Root Cause

When Diamondhead Corporation started to steer Pinehurst in the 1970s, the town feared the new ownership group would discard a lot of the rich history that made Pinehurst tick.

The annals of the early days of Pinehurst were going to be sent to the dump, and one of the staunchest opponents of this move was by Pinehurst resident Fred Heanlin. Some of the documents that were headed to the dumpster included information on the early cottages (1895-1921) on Cherokee Road in Pinehurst. Heanlin rescued the information and began compiling his study on the various cottages. "There is more history in the early development and the cottages than anyone cares to admit," said Heanlin, shortly before his death in 2003. He said, "It is fascinating to understand how the village was comprised. When Pinehurst first started, the life blood lived in these cottages."

Heanlin, along with several Pinehurst residents, prevented Diamondhead from discarding valuable maps, cottage locations and owners' information. Heanlin then started accumulating the information on the cottages in the late 1980s and worked on the project consistently for more than 10 years. One of Heanlin's friends during his research was John Root. Root, 60, came to Pinehurst "because we had friends that lived here, and it was the latitude we were looking for." Retired, Root also got interested in how the original village was comprised. They met and had several discussions on the history of Pinehurst. "We basically were interested in the same thing; how the early days of Pinehurst evolved," said Root. He adds, "The initial discussions started because I realized the roads over here [the village] were not the same as the ones near the golf courses."

When Heanlin died, he bequeathed the research to Root to continue. "I have developed a map, and the work is really a compilation of past owners, names and nicknames of cottages [some which have changed over the years]."

One of Heanlin's last actions included getting pictures of the cottages. The old adage "Success is not a destination, but a journey," applies to the historical content he compiled. "I hope to add to his study, but I don't know if it will ever be complete," Root said.

September 11, 1974

Bill Collett was the professional at Inwood Forest Country Club in Houston. In 1971, he ventured to Pinehurst to the PGA Club Professional's Championship where he met Bill Maurer, the head of Diamondhead Corp., then the proud owner of Pinehurst.

The two minds were interested in a common purpose; creating a Golf Hall of Fame. Maurer and Collett talked about several possible locations, which included Atlanta, Pebble Beach, Pinehurst and San Diego as possible sites for the permanent home.

Collett then traveled to Cooperstown and Canton. He talked with the then-presidents of the Pro Football Hall of Fame and the Baseball Hall of Fame. Both organizations explained the pitfalls of the early years. Collett came away with one rule: Don't put too much effort into raising money and not enough effort into how you are going to keep the money flowing once the doors are open.

Part of Collett's drive in establishing the Hall had to do with being a friend of Billy Casper. Both men played for the golf team at the Naval Air Station in the 1950s. Collett co-authored a book with the 1959 U.S. Open Champion, and he wanted a place for Casper's career highlights and his putter once his career was punctuated.

Maurer and Diamondhead contributed a reported $2.5 million. The dream was starting to become reality—or was it?

The Hall of Fame finally opened on September 11, 1974. Somehow Collett managed to attract President Ford, who had taken office one month previously following the Watergate scandal. Thirteen enshrinees were welcomed into the Hall: Arnold Palmer, Jack Nicklaus, Ben Hogan, Sam Snead, Byron Nelson, Gary Player, Gene Sarazen, Patty Berg, Harry Vardon, Babe Didrikson Zaharias, Frances Ouimet, Bobby Jones and Walter Hagen.

The Golf Hall of Fame stayed open for 20 years behind the fourth green of the No. 2 course. The roof leaked and the attendance was spry.

Deane Beman made it part of his agenda in the mid-1980s to address the failing institution. Some call it a breakfast ball, others call it a second chance. What happened was Beman got with former LPGA commissioner Charlie Mechem and they proposed a mulligan—called the World Golf Village. The location, somewhere close to PGA headquarters, eventually opened 30 minutes south of Jacksonville, Florida,. in St. Augustine.

St. Augustine lacked the historical aura of Pinehurst, but since it was the oldest city in America, they thought it had a marketing presence. And one of the concepts for the organizers was to provide a progressive environment that would keep growing with the times, and possibly the long-term vision that prevented the Pinehurst Hall of Fame from its loss of trajectory.

They initially designed the expansion of the entire complex to take place on more than 6,300 acres. This included a golf course, which will eventually house a Senior PGA event, a PGA Tour-sanctioned golf academy and a hotel and convention center.

A lot of people made their way to Pinehurst; the Golf Hall of Fame was an afterthought. People came to play golf; they passed the Hall, only by making their way from the fourth green to the fifth tee. The date of its opening, the location, the architectural design of the building and the overall combination led to what is now just pine trees behind the fourth green.

7

More Than
Just a Course

For some, Pinehurst No. 2 has become more than just a golf course. Here are some opinions from the philosophers and the greatest players of all time.

Tony Penna—"It's a golf course built by God, and Donald Ross knew how to take advantage of nature. There is nothing synthetic about Pinehurst."

Paul Azinger—"You want to play more than 18 holes."

Bill Coore, partner with Ben Crenshaw in golf course design—"Its greatness really eludes people at first unless they're well versed in golf-course design; the little things, the angles, contouring work around the greens, the bunkers. All that goes together to make it the whole that it is."

Ben Crenshaw—"Pinehurst may be the best championship course in the whole world."

Charles Price—"No. 2 is one of the best courses because not a single hole is out of character with the rest. The result ought to somehow be declared a national treasure.

Executive director of the USGA David Fay—"Quite simply the best golf course in the world."

Carole Semple Thompson, long-time USGA board member and amateur champion—"The course really doesn't favor any one player, because it calls for such diverse shot making, such as accurate driving, a superb short game and a knowledge of the greens and how they fit into the contour of the land."

Ben Hogan—"[It is] the best golf course because of the way it fits into the land."

Sam Snead—"Pinehurst No. 2 is just behind the Upper Cascades course, because almost all the other great golf courses had at least one relatively weak hole. The 18th at Cypress Point, the 10th at Merion, the 17th at Oakmont. Pinehurst does not have one weak hole."

More Than a Resort

In the early years, the Pinehurst resort was marketed as a local winter retreat. Early marketing was unique, an ideal place in which to spend the winter, where the climate is perfection and where outdoor life is ideal: four fine hotels ranging in price from $2.50 per day upward, excellent preparatory school, the best golf courses (two of them) in the South, with frequent tournaments, a 35,000-acre shooting preserve, tennis courts, a livery of fine saddle horses, etc., and the only village in the South from which consumptives are excluded. Other material exposed Pinehurst as the "winter golf center of America."

On June 13, 1921, noted golf course architect of Pinehurst, Donald Ross, sent a letter to Pinehurst founder

Leonard Tufts, in which he wrote his recommendation for the newfound sport in America—golf. He said succinctly that "We should play strong on the outdoor recreation that is becoming more and more a part of American life. I have laid out nine new 18-hole courses, which proves catering to the American love of outdoor life is becoming a leading and important business." A century later Ross's instincts are strangely accurate.

The Only Game in Town

To reduce Pinehurst to a singular game would be simple art. After all, simple art best defines the canvas of Pinehurst No. 2 and its painter, Donald Ross. And steering the golf ball through mammoth pines to smallish greens that repel poor shots is the main game on the Pinehurst campus. It is truly another game that should receive top billing. It actually takes place in the hotel, once owned by Ross.

I'm talking about the chipping board at the tiny Pine Crest Inn. The chipping board represents all that is truly Pinehurst. A tee time, 18 holes of golf, dinner and sleep is not Pinehurst. Pinehurst is about a process of absorption. It begins somewhere along Highway 5 heading into the business district. Pinehurst is all about slowing your body movements to a leisurely pass, dropping the heart rate a few beats per minute and taking in the canopy of greenery that surrounds the village. And it is about this chipping board. Why? Because this venue at the Pine Crest is where tales are told, rounds are revisited, memories retold and the true spirit of the game enhanced. For sure, there are typically other forms of spirits in hand when the board comes alive. But the very essence of the town, the game and the lifestyle of Pinehurst are captured here.

In the early 1960s Lionel Callaway built the original chipping board that consisted of a piece of plywood with a foam frame. The hole in the plywood measured eight inches in diameter. Callaway would hold putting and chipping instruction clinics in the Pine Crest lobby. The chipping board allowed him to simulate the proper way to pinch the ball off tight lies. The original board lasted until the night of Hurricane Fran in 1996. The Barrett family, owners of the Pine Crest, still remember the fateful day the chipping board

The No. 2 course served as the stage for play in the 1999 U.S. Open. (Photo provided by the Pinehurst Convention and Visitors Bureau.)

was taken. "We lost power, several trees and the chipping board the same night," said Andee Hoffman, wife of Bobby Barrett. The loss of the chipping board was lessened by the reconstruction of a new, improved board made by the hotel's maintenance staff. The games vary each night, but the usual contest involves what is deemed a free-throw line. That area, approximately eight feet from the board, serves as the tee box. The board, which sits in front of the lobby fireplace, might be the busiest course at Pinehurst.

Callaway was a club maker, an inventor, a writer and an overall ambassador of the game. However, his greatest invention might be the chipping board.

The Inn's staff does not keep statistics on the chipping board, but they believe Ben Crenshaw to have the record for the most consecutive made chips at the Pine Crest. Michael Jordan has afforded a few games at the chipping board. And so did Payne Stewart during his 1999 U.S. Open run. Countless other athletes have all experienced Pinehurst by way of the chipping board as well. NBA and NCAA basketball coaches have wagered a few pesos on the ability to sink a few drinks and the golf ball from downtown. Ask Chuck Daly, Kevin Loughery, Dean Smith, and Bill Raftery about the chipping board, and a wide grin erupts on their faces.

At night, when the chipping board comes alive, is when all errant shots and contests take center stage. As a watering hole, the Pine Crest has more than a storied reputation. Travelers including the best amateurs and professionals in the game compete at the Pine Crest. For some it is a way to pass the evening hours until the next day's early tee time. For others it becomes a golfing casino with wagers ranging from 50 cents up to thousands of dollars. The Callaway Chipping Board is a national treasure; the same way the No. 2 course remains a signature landmark in a game that is timeless.

Sitting above the mantle of the fireplace is a picture of Donald Ross. Not too far in the distance is a picture of Payne Stewart.

No. 2

Donald Ross died in 1948 after several successful golf course design efforts. Yet when his legacy is fully academically examined, the one glaring defining course that stands out is Pinehurst's No. 2. The Tufts family loved the course because it mirrored "the conditions and designs of those in Scotland." Those who tested their game on No. 2 were befuddled and bewitched by the seemingly simple course that dared those players to take dead aim at the small greens with mid to long-irons in their hands. "You must play it with your head as much as your hands," said Johnny Revolta. Paul Azinger noted, "The place [No.2] is much like Augusta, you have to know where to put the ball on the greens." And a player who has one green jacket, Fred Couples, said, "In a tournament, you just try to make pars at No. 2, because you know par is a decent score."

The Short Grass

The comparison between Pinehurst and Augusta National has been going on for some years. Jack Nicklaus says, "The only real comparison that is fair is that they probably have the two toughest sets of greens that I know. And I think Pinehurst's are more difficult than Augusta, the way they have changed the green edges, and have taken the edges off. They are the smallest-playing large greens, good-sized greens that I've ever seen. There is really not much to play to." Nicklaus, a more than established course designer himself, acknowledges Ross's brilliance, but says, "Nobody can complain too much about it, because Donald Ross is no longer around." Tiger Woods, after playing the final 18 in the 1999 U.S. Open, said, "The greens were slower than normal, but what makes Pinehurst more severe than Augusta is the mounds." Pinehurst greens superintendent Paul Jett says, "I think Pinehurst stands the test of time so well because of the greens. Nobody is scared playing this golf course from tee to fairway. I think this golf course will stand for many years because you're never going to be able to get every shot hit exactly where it needs to be hit. With certain pin placements and different conditions, you have to be precise with the irons; and then if you're not, then the chipping and putting game has to be exceptional. And Ross was no dummy, and he knew what he was doing as any great architect did and will do."

And as the U.S. Open and other majors fight the improvements and changes in the game, Ross's design offers a European links look to a totally small-town American venue.

Tim Morgaghan of the USGA said at the U.S. Open in 1999, "I think Pinehurst is so similar to what the players encounter on the other side of the ocean. I think that was Ross's intention when he came over here." And Ross was brilliant in his definition of one rare element of the game— putting. Ross once said, "The contouring around a green makes possible an infinite variety in the requirements for short shots that no other hazard can call for." Rees Jones, who tweaked the course for the 1999 U.S. Open says, "Pinehurst No. 2 is sacred ground in golf, and it's his [Ross's] hands on creation."

The Angst

Tommy Armour said, "The man who doesn't feel emotionally stirred when he plays golf at Pinehurst beneath the blue Carolina skies and with the pine fragrance in his nostrils...This is the man that should be ruled out of golf for life. It's the kind of course that gets into the blood of an old trooper."

The Ryder Cup

Maybe it was the state of the game in 1951. The world's best golfers came to Pinehurst for the Ryder Cup matches. Captained by Sam Snead, the team consisted of such notables as Skip Alexander, Jack Burke, Lloyd Mangrum, Henry Ransom, Ben Hogan, Clayton Heafner and Porky Oliver. Several journalists from Britain did not understand the smallish crowds in central North Carolina. One such writer asked a local for the reason the crowds numbered less than 5,000 spectators. The answer: "Are you aware of the players on the other courses? In Pinehurst, *everyone* plays golf."

Billy Joe Patton

"There is no one I can compare him to in golf today," said Bill Campbell about his long-time friend and amateur partner, Billy Joe Patton.

Campbell knows Patton's career at Pinehurst and in amateur circles better than anyone. But it is a story off the course that Campbell likes to tell.

"He was a favorite of President Eisenhower. He used to play golf and bridge with the president," offered Campbell. "And Billy Joe was from Morganton, NC, you know, a country soul. Patton was asked to come to Washington, D.C. for a political dinner. He was a guest and he met 22 other couples at this dinner, often meeting the spouses of each couple separately. He always seemed to be aloof and not really paying attention at the social event. He met most of the people individually and for the first time. But at the end of the night he offered a proper introduction and thanks to all 22 couples, mixing up only one couple."

Campbell says that Patton was an outstanding player, "but he didn't always drive the ball the straightest."

Patton won three North and South titles but is probably best known for the chance that got away at the 1954 Masters. Long-time Pinehurst resident John Derr wrote: "It started in the 14th tee during the fourth round of the 1954

Master. It probably started long before that, but without the national sports media, which that week had taken the talented young Tar Heel to its bosom at Augusta National."

As an invitational event, the 1953 Masters committee, headed by Clifford Roberts and Bob Jones, made some changes. They elected to invite the U.S. and Great Britain Walker Cup members. This group happened to include an invite to a certain Morganton, NC, resident, William J. (Billy Joe) Patton.

Derr writes, "In those days there was no Wednesday play of the Masters Par Three course: it had not been built. Instead, Wednesday spectators were treated to a long-driving contest. Balls were driven into the area between the eighth and the 18th fairways.

"Patton limbered up and took his place in the tee box. Handed the three balls that each competitor could hit, he teed one up and reared back. Off it went into orbit, causing the official markers to retreat, and they sent word that Patton had driven the first ball 335 yards, as I recall. Billy Joe tossed the other two balls down and walked away. No one else even came close."

Patton was not done yet.

Patton led the Masters after 36 holes, the first amateur to lead the event at this point. He was even par, one ahead of Ben Hogan and two ahead of Sam Snead. After a third-round 75, he trailed Hogan by five and Snead by two.

The final round was highlighted by the Walker Cup alternate's even-par start. At the par-three sixth, Patton pulled out a 5-iron, and his shot came to rest nestled against the flagstick. He questioned USGA rules official Joe Dey on whether he could touch the flagstick. He carefully pulled the flagstick away, allowing him to witness the ball toppling into the hole for an ace. The azaleas and dogwoods were rocking. Patton added birdies at eight and nine, which left him with a final-round outgoing 32. Patton was leading the Masters with nine to play. As everyone has come to understand, the Masters was really just beginning.

But it was the crucial second shot on the 13th that proved to be his undoing. He tried to carry the creek. He failed, carded a seven and eventually finished two strokes out of a playoff with Snead who finished at 289, well in front of Patton and Hogan. Hogan wound up tied with Snead. Snead won the playoff by a single stroke (71-70).

Patton at Pinehurst

Maybe it was a match with Hobart Manley Jr. in 1951 that really was the difference in Billy Joe Patton becoming a legend. It was because of this match with Manley that Herbert Warren Wind declared, "Billy Joe Patton was like a breath of fresh air. There is no one like him."

A native of Georgia, Manley enjoyed life on and off the course. On the eighth hole in their finals match, Manley sent his drive into the woods on the left. Manley was not near the ball, when it apparently moved on some pine needles. Thinking this was an infraction, Manley indicated to Patton he was lying three as he pitched the ball back into play. Manley pitched the ball close and made what he felt was a bogey. Patton played the hole conservatively, made par for what he thought was a winning hole. The rules official asked Manley what had happened in the woods, and after a discussion it was deemed to be a tied hole, since the ball moved before Manley had addressed it. Manley felt awful. Patton remarked at the turn, "Get me a Coke and forget about it." Manley didn't forget about it.

When they got to the 14th tee, Patton led Manley two-up. That is when Manley went on a birdie (14), par (15), eagle (16), par (17) birdie (18) binge to seal the win.

Patton ironically would get his chance at redemption a little more than a decade later. In the 1962 North and South, the two met again in the finals. This time it was all Patton. He won seven and six.

Patton's loss to Labron E. Harris in the semifinals of the 1962 U.S. Amateur is one that he would like to have back. Even though he won three North and South titles, the U.S. Amateur eluded him.

On April 29, 1963, Richard Tufts said, "I honestly don't see how a man could do better than that. I have serious doubts that this performance has ever been surpassed in amateur golf, unless maybe by Lawson Little when he won both the U.S. and British Amateur titles the same year."

Patton had just beaten Bob Allen to win the North and South back to back. He won 19 of 20 matches on the No. 2 course (his only loss to Harris in the U.S. Amateur semis).

During one North and South match, Patton was trying to play his second from out of the woods (which was the norm). As the crowd grew silent, one of the ladies said, "The hotel said I'm losing my room tonight." Patton backed away and said, "Don't worry, if I miss this shot, you can have mine."

Bobby Jones

Bobby Jones, the player noted for the Impregnable Quadrilateral of 1930, showed up at Pinehurst in 1932 after almost 15 years removed from the fairways at Pinehurst. He was busy preparing a course down the road in Georgia. In a column written by Harry Yorke, he said, "Our club in Augusta is to be restricted to 1,000 members. We expect to have 500 to 600 as an average count for the opening years, and to reach 1,000 inside of five years. Dr. MacKenzie has laid out a perfectly magnificent course. We have without doubt the four best one-shot holes in any course I've ever seen. On every hole the pitch shot is entirely different, due to the green construction. We have a water sprinkler system which alone cost $40,000. Grass greens are patterned after the famous greens of St. Andrews in Scotland."

And so, the reason Bobby Jones showed up in 1932 might have been to compare his Augusta track to the Pinehurst track.

Yorke writes, "Bobby waved that wand over the obdurate No. 2 course, and lo, a round for two below par was the result!"

Yorke said he intercepted Jones on the 14th tee on the second day to ask, "How are you doing?"

The response from Jones, "Pretty well, a couple under fours."

Jones's trip to Pinehurst in 1932 was part of an exhibition that was common in the day. He was helping introduce a new paintless golf ball by Spaulding & Brothers.

The advent of the paintless ball was part of a tour with Jones, Japanese champion Tamaki Miyamoto, U.S. Open Champion Billy Burke and Bill Mehlhorn.

Jones spent two days playing golf and bunking at the Carolina Hotel.

8

The Old
and the Young

"If I were home I'd almost be getting out of science class and going to social studies in 10 minutes, no, five minutes, sorry," said Morgan Pressel. Morgan Pressel is the youngest player to have qualified to compete in the U.S. Women's Open. She arrived in Pinehurst in May of 2001 to compete with the best players in the world. Her grandfather was the one who led her to attempt to qualify for the Open. "He said he was going to play at Bear Lakes [the site of the qualifier] and I said, 'Okay, for what?' And he said, 'The U.S. Open.' And I just said, 'I'm going to make it.'"

Willie McRae

Willie McRae is the oldest living caddy at Pinehurst. He started caddying in 1943, and at the ripe age of 68, was a perfect selection to be paired with Pressel for the 2001 U.S. Women's Open. "I was really surprised I got such a good caddy," said Pressel. "He's one of 10 caddies in the Pinehurst Caddy Hall of Fame." And so Pressel (age 12) and McRae (age 68) formed a team to take on Pine Needles.

Pressel did not make the cut at Pine Needles, but her visage did appear on the Pinehurst phone book the following year.

Jack Nicklaus

Jack Nicklaus walked into the press room at the 1999 U.S. Open with the same confident stare that he brought to Inverness in 1959 as a 17-year-old kid playing in his first U.S. Open. "I remember I was leading the tournament after three holes. I holed a 35-footer for a birdie on the first hole, and I parred the next two holes—never to be seen again." Well, we know better. Nicklaus was not seen on the radar anymore that week, but he did go on to win four U.S. Opens.

Forty years earlier he had visited Pinehurst and shot over 80 in his final two rounds to win the North and South. In 1959, Nicklaus was a pudgy kid from southern Ohio with a game that held promise. He remembers the North and South as a brutal test. "The greens were as hard as rocks. If you hit the ball off line you could get in a hole or sand and it would just bounce in a bunch of different directions. Today they work so hard to get the condition of the golf course more uniform and consistent. Some of the shots that were unfair and some of the bad shots from those days just do not happen anymore, mostly because of the technology we have the ability to reduce the course down." The North and South is a special place for the Nicklaus family. Jack's son Jackie played Tom McKnight in the finals of the North and South. Before the match, McKnight remembers the

Golden Bear walking up to him. "He looked at me and introduced himself as Jack Nicklaus," said McKnight. "As if I didn't know who he was."

Nicklaus turned professional just as the resort hosted the 1964 U.S. Amateur and returned in 1999 at one of his last majors. The best golfer in the last 100 years has a word of warning for the players as they prepare to return to Pinehurst in 2005. "If you look at the game since I've been playing it, the game has changed a whole bunch. Not much before I started playing it, they were playing with wooden shafts and with a small ball. And then they were playing with smaller heads, wood heads. I don't know where they

From left to right, a young Jack Nicklaus along with William B. Foreman and runner-up Gene Andrews.

are going to go with it next. I think they've made the game much easier for the average golfer; too easy for the competitive golfer. And where they will go from here, I don't know. I certainly think there needs to be a harness on it some place."

Simon Hobday

When you think of South African players winning U.S. Opens, the name Ernie Els enters the conversation. And in 1994, Els had just won his first Open title when a fellow South African showed up at Pinehurst. His fellow Senior PGA Tour players call him "Scruffy." That's because in a tournament in South Africa early in his career, he had a shoe "that broke." So he said, "I had to borrow a shoe from one of my pals. It just happened to be a brown shoe, and the other shoe was black. So, I played the tournament like that, but my name Scruffy stuck because I had one black shoe and one brown shoe."

Simon Hobday likes to fish. So after his first round at Pinehurst, in the U.S. Senior Open, he decided to take up the owner of the Magnolia Inn's offer to take a mate out on a little lake and throw a line in. The fish were not biting at first, so Scruffy used the proverbial open bathroom off the side of the boat. Next thing he knew, his mate shifted weight and Scruffy was swampy. "I was swimming next to it to get the boat back to the bank. I tell you there were a lot of snakes in that water too. Those buggers were as thick as your arms in there." And while Hobday's number-one experience on the boat left him pondering other fishing trips, his effort on No. 2 down the road left Graham Marsh and Jim Albus playing for second place. From the back nine on Thursday, through play on Saturday, Hobday was executing his game to perfection. Using a 4-wood occasionally around the greens, Holiday was the sort of fellow who showed up at the 1994 U.S. Senior Open on Pinehurst No. 2 with not an inkling of the championship in his mind. In 1982, he quit playing the European circuit because he was tired. He decided to enter the car alarm business. "We were turning over something like $500,000 a month, so we were going. It was a good business." This was not Hobday's most unusual profession. After all, he was a cattle rancher and farmer in the early 1960s.

Then Simon Hobday turned 50, and a player by the name of Harold Henning said to give golf another try. So Hobday gave it a try and he has amassed more money on the Senior PGA Tour than he ever did cattle ranching or selling car alarms.

And with a closing-round 75, Hobday was not exactly happy about his final round.

"I was terrible and my swing deserted me. I was lucky to hit a few bad putts that went in the hole. I was very fortunate."

Orcutt and Collett

In 1922, a 17-year-old girl from Englewood, NJ was introduced to golf. Once she was given the basics, Maureen Orcutt was ignited with a passion to be the best golfer ever. Her mother baited her by acknowledging; "If you can beat me, you can have my club membership [White Beeches Golf Club in Haworth, NJ]." That was all she needed to hear. She was a quick study in swinging the hickory-shafted clubs and won the New Jersey state title in less than six months. As a senior at Englewood High School, she skipped final exams to win the Women's Eastern Amateur. And she was just getting started on a whirlwind spree of success.

She won 10 Metropolitan Amateur titles, seven Eastern Amateur crowns, and made several trips to the sand region of Pinehurst. And yes, she played when there was actually sand on the greens in Pinehurst.

Orcutt was adept at being the center of the story on the golf course, but during an amateur career that spanned four decades, she would also write about the story from the sports desk at the *New York Times*.

Orcutt began her newspaper work at the *New York Journal*, then the *New York World* and eventually joined the *New York Times* on the sports desk in 1937. Nicknamed "the Duchess," she would oftentimes cover events in which she competed, all the while keeping the objective journalistic point of view. She retired in Durham, North Carolina.

Her trips to Pinehurst were legendary. A local reporter said, "Her game is brilliant and her personality is colorful."

Her golf led her into circles that not many amateurs have ventured. She claimed three North and South titles in the 1930s and then collected three Senior North and South titles in the 1960s. She made it to two U.S. Amateur finals (1927, 1936), but lost both times. Her track record led her to be a member of the first ever Curtis Cup matches in 1932. The U.S. beat the Great Britain/Ireland team five and one half to three and one half. She was also a member of the winning efforts in 1934, 1936 and 1938. Her match record of (2-0-1) in foursomes and (3-1-1) in singles is among the best ever in the competition.

Orcutt became part of a unique foursome in the 1930s and 1940s that included Glenna Collett Vare, Helen Hicks and Virginia Van Wie.

Collett, like Orcutt, was a big hitter. Similar to Orcutt, she was introduced to the game by her father at the age of 16 in 1919. Compared to Bobby Jones, Collett was dominant at a time when the sport was gaining momentum, and she was a driving force on the development of the women's game. She ended her career with six U.S. Amateur titles, from 1922 to 1935, including the most lopsided victory in the history of the event at the Homestead, (Hot Springs, VA) beating Virginia Van Wie 13 and 12. When she won her last U.S. Amateur in 1935, she beat Patty Berg three and two.

Collett was instrumental in organizing the Curtis Cup matches and was part of the American effort in the first six (1932-1950). She was named the winner of the prestigious Bob Jones Award in 1965.

Collett and Orcutt never won a single professional event, but they paved the way for Patty Berg, Mickey Wright, Nancy Lopez, Karrie Webb and Annika Sorrenstam.

Jett also worked closely with the USGA to provide the best championship venue available for the 1999 U.S. Open and all other major amateur championships that are hosted at No. 2.

If Jett has only been around Pinehurst since 1995, how does he know the heritage of what Ross set out to accomplish? "I remember looking at photos of Ross's work without the benefits of an irrigation system. What he dealt with was immeasurable. We have better grasses, better mowers. If we have problems with the golf course, we can call university people that can give us answers. It is a different business than even 10 years ago, let alone 100 years ago."

No. 1

In the 1949 North and South Open, Sam Snead knocked his second shot to within two feet for a birdie on his way to an opening-round 66 and eventually the title. Ross once said that the opening hole of any course should not be too difficult—"Give the player a chance to warm up." he said. The opening hole at No. 2 is just that. But there is a theme that begins at the first. Do not miss the target green. Jett calls the first hole a trademark Donald Ross "handshake hole." Hank Kuehne doesn't think it is a handshake hole. Kuehne played the first hole in nine over par, including two triple bogeys (rounds two and three) during the 1997 Open. Jett says, "It's not too difficult unless you hit it in the left bunker, and then any number is possible."

9

The Outward Nine

M ost successful golf teachers have the capacity to get
the individual to groove a swing. Leadbetter, Smith,
Harmon...they all know square to square, but when it comes
to course management, No. 2 provides an Einsteinish equation on...well, let's ponder the choices. Do we bump and
run or toss a flop? Is there reward in being short or long?
Would I rather take my chances from a greenside bunker or
shaved collar? Long-time Pinehurst caddie Jeff Ferguson said,
"It's really a mid-iron golf course. Miss it [the green] in the
right places or else. "The toughest holes on the golf course
are one through six. That determines your round."

There is really no better way to take a tour of the best
golf course in the land than to listen to every word from the
person who directs the efforts of manicuring the No. 2
course, course superintendent Paul Jett. Since 1995, Jett has
made it his responsibility to make sure the course provides a
fair test for the world's best amateur and professional players. Jett said, "I agree that the toughest holes are the early
holes."

No. 2

At the 1999 U.S. Open, Greg Norman said the second hole is where you get a real lesson on the convex greens at Pinehurst. The second hole was the sixth most difficult during the event with a 4.4 stroke average. Davis Love III says the second hole is where you pull out the driver and bust it. It is best to keep the ball on the left side of the fairway to get the best angle to approach the green. Jett said, "I wish we could get the tee farther back so that the bunkers come into play. Right now they are just aiming bunkers. Don't pay too much attention to the drive, because the green complex at two is one of the three most difficult on the course. Fifteen, five and two would be the top three." Pin placement on the second makes a difference; back middle and back right can create havoc. Miss it long and the Pinehurst dilemma begins: what club to use to get the ball back on the green.

You can't worry about getting the ball to the hole until you get it to the green. Ferguson calls the second green the toughest on the golf course. Welcome to No. 2 on No. 2.

No. 3

This may very well be known as the Payne Stewart hole. This is the short par four where Stewart made three birdies in four rounds during his championship run in 1999. Not the most difficult in terms of length, the third requires another target approach shot. The advantage goes to a creative player who can manufacture greenside shots. This is where the three words "up and in" start to resonate. Jett reminds the player, "The waste area behind the green is not where you want to be. But at Pinehurst, long is not where you want to be on any hole. If you aren't smart, you'll end up with five here."

No. 4

This was the easiest hole in the 1999 U.S. Open. Most players used an iron off the tee to get into an approach position. Hitting over this green leaves the player few choices.

To call this a sleeper hole would not be fitting, but the fourth might be the Wednesday of the front nine. What kind of score one gets here usually dictates what's next. It is a brutal stretch of power and precision. "If you're going to make a birdie on the front nine, this is a good place to start," Jett says.

No. 5

Only 27 percent of the field hit this par four in two during the Open. Assuming you hit a great tee shot, you're left with a long approach shot off a side hill lie. Missing the green left creates more than a troubling chip to another difficult green. On this hole, left is wrong. Steer right on the approach and hope your ball rests on the putting surface. Right and short of the green is great! In the late 1970s and early 1980s, a shot short left of this green meant it would roll all the way down the slope. What's left? An impossible chip. Jett said, "Donald Ross's house is just to the right of the fifth green. Three and five are the top two greatest greens complexes on the golf course. I'm talking about the total green complex, not just taking the greens, but the bunkers, the slope behind the green and everything into account. I can picture him [Ross] coming out there and hitting balls. Because he lived there and he saw those two greens more than any other, that is why those two greens are what they are. I watched a bunch of players in 1999 hit five and six irons into the green. At No. 2 you have to know how far you have to hit it, you have to know the break in the green, because the greens repel poorly played shots." This hole will reward a great shot.

No. 6

Long-time caddie Charlie McRae calls the sixth hole the defining hole on the golf course. "Both professionals and amateurs try and get the ball to the pin off the tee.

What I try to encourage is a well-played shot to the front of the green. This leaves most players, especially the amateur players, a great chance to make par." A greedy player invites a double bogey on this challenging par three. With a directional change on the golf course, both holes five and six create a premium on club selection. Some say the wind is always in your face at Pinehurst. This hole can be a real test depending on the Carolina breeze. Mostly surrounded by trees, this hole can have a swirling wind, which makes club selection difficult. It played as the toughest par three on the golf course in 1999. The green sits at a difficult angle to the tee so that a low shot usually rolls off the green and catches the front bunker. "One out of four amateur players hit the ball in the left bunker usually," Jett said.

No. 7

Off the tee, the play is a 250-yard, fairway wood or two iron. After that, the approach shot is one of the most challenging on the course. This is one of the tougher green complexes.

A dramatic pitch right to left, which makes your precision approach shot difficult to hold with a green falling away. The green is bunkered and it is kind of like hitting an egg to a plate being propped up by a coffee mug.

No. 8

When the USGA's Tom Meeks, Tim Moraghan and Jett met in 1998 to discuss course strategy, all three men decided with hesitation that eight would play as a par four. After all, it had played as a par four for the last 15 years of championship golf.

But John Daly's 11 on this hole in the final round is indicative of how this can turn into a chipping nightmare if your approach shot blows over the green. Following the event, Daly said he hit a perfect 6-iron onto the green.

Jett said, "It wasn't a perfect 6-iron because it went over the back of the green. That is one of the things you have to know in order to play this course. One of the rules at No. 2 is you cannot be over the back of the eighth green. If you're faced with this dilemma, you have to hit something [one of 14 clubs] to get back on the putting surface."

No. 9

No. 9 is as difficult a one-shot hole as there is on the No. 2 course. Just ask David Duval about his experience playing this par three. His final-round charge to Stewart and Mickelson was derailed on this hole when he was forced to play out of the bunker. Jett said, "The bunkers here are very penal if you get in them. Most players will play a 6- or 7-iron to the middle of the green, grab par and get out."

The Inward Nine

No. 10

If there is a true three-shot par five on No. 2, this is it. It is a great beginning to the inward half. Both Tiger Woods and John Daly were hole-high during play in 1999, but the average length player is left with a wedge shot onto the green. The importance of the third shot was displayed in the final round of the Open. Both Payne Stewart and Phil Mickelson played poor shots onto this green. Mickelson's shot hit a slope and went into the bunker, out of which he made par. Stewart spun his ball back off the green. He settled for a bogey. Many players lick their chops at getting off to a birdie start on the back nine.

No. 11

No. 11 is the only hole on the golf course with a nickname—Hogan's Alley. Ben Hogan referenced the hole as "the best flat par four [he] ever played." This after Hogan recorded his first professional win at Pinehurst. Miss the fairway right and you end up in the Pinehurst waste area—hardpan sand, wiregrass and pine needles. Because of the angle of the green, the approach shot needs to be juxtaposed vs. the pin location. It is another subtle "thinking player's" hole. This begins a stretch of four straight par fours.

No. 12

The 12th was lengthened before the 1999 U.S. Open. "Because the hole plays downwind most of the time, we felt that the added length might not make a big difference for the Open," Jett said. Wrong. "That hole played into the wind every day of the 1999 event." The hole invites a left-center fairway location, which affords the player the best way to attack the green.

No. 13

No. 13 is the second shortest par four on the course, but don't let the length fool you. This hole repelled more shots during the 1999 U.S. Open and left players scrambling for par with chip shots to a crowded green. Depending on pin placement, this hole can be demanding. The exactness of the approach makes this a win-lose proposition. A birdie here by Stewart on Sunday propelled him to the championship. This is where he went from even to one under on the back nine.

No. 14

The tees will be coming back on this hole for the 2005 Open. "We will build a tee that is specifically for the Open. Right now, for players in the North and South, it is a driver and an eight iron," Jett said. But lengthening the hole will add to its demanding characteristics.

No. 15

The fun part about 15 is the greens complex. "We got with the USGA on what length to leave the areas around our greens in 1998, just prior to the Open," said Jett. "What happened was that we settled on a height that provided the player the option to play different types of shots from the same location. We did not want it too low and tight where the only option was the putter." Like at the sixth, playing up to this green keeps par in the equation. Playing from over the green brings a lot of numbers into the mix. "The play on this hole is middle of the green which, depending on pin location, leaves a 25-foot birdie putt," Jett said. Par is a great score on 15 with three demanding holes left.

No. 16

The USGA's Tom Meeks showed up at the 1998 Men's North and South specifically to sit behind the 16th green for two days and chart the players' shots. Meeks evaluated the irons they were hitting into the green and the players' success in making par. The hole was played both as a par four and a par five during qualifying. "That was the driving force for us playing the hole as a par four," Jett said. The hole was played at 489 yards. This hole was also part of the discussions the USGA had with Jett on rough height. "We actually had done some tests of test plots of rough prior to the 1999 event. We did three inches, four inches and five inches to determine what length would best allow the player to advance the ball toward the greens. Jack Nicklaus had been in Pinehurst the week prior to the event and said, 'If the rough was a little lower, it would allow the player a better chance to advance it.' What we settled on was four inches, which we felt was a good length for the tournament." As far as the greens complex, this one is no cupcake. Making the 16th a par four really adds some beef to the backside and makes the finishing holes something special. The putt he made on 16 was the best of the three. Unless you stand and look at that putt, no one has any idea how difficult that putt really is. It has two breaks in it and it is downhill. He probably could have stood there with a small bucket and not made more than one, but all he needed was that one.

No. 17

Pin placement plays a role in how aggressive the player can be. This hole set up beautifully for a Payne Stewart 7-iron. It could be argued that it was the shot of the tournament. Wind direction and club selection here make this an exacting approach shot. The length of the hole is not what makes the 17th a difficult hole. The combination of a convex angled green and hungry bunkers make this a beast.

No. 18

Jett said, "Stewart was rewarded for playing the 18th smart. Instead of trying to challenge the rough, he made the play that left him with a makeable putt to win the golf tournament. Jett has two or three cup-cutters that find a spot close to where Stewart's 15-foot putt rolled every Sunday.

"They cut the cup there, and we use a flag for that pin that shows him in a pose as he made that putt, with the inscription 'One Moment in Time,'" Jett said.

While Jett continues to prepare the course, his main objective in the coming months is to get 25 bunkers resodded, shaped and contoured for tournament play. "The course is going to be a different course in 2005, it will be six years older, I will need to get the green rolling as well as I can, get the areas around the green as firm as possible. It is likely we will have a totally different weather scenario in 2005 as well," Jett said.

One thing he knows for sure: "We want to make those areas around the greens the big story. That is where we are going to find our champion."

Be My Guest

"Tis good to go to Boston, Tis sweet to stop at Rye. But I would go to Pinehurst where all the golf balls fly."

— "At Pinehurst" by Edgar A. Guest.

He was "the poet of the people" because he wrote about everyday life. In 1895, the same year Pinehurst was clearing land and starting to build, Guest was a 13-year-old office boy for the *Detroit Free Press*. He ended up staying with the paper for 60 years. In the early years he had the job of cutting timeless items from the sister papers of the *Free Press*. And he figured out quickly that he might as well come up with some of his own verse and submit it to the Sunday editor, Arthur Moseley. Moseley hesitantly decided to publish his first verse on December 11, 1898. This led to a weekly column and time as a reporter. Guest earned the reputation of a scrappy reporter in a town that rewarded such work.

After 10 years of submitting to the grind of daily reporting in a competitive town, Guest turned back to his verse and never let go.

His time in Pinehurst was best used to contemplate life's daily happenings. It led to several poems, which his brother Harry helped him typeset. Before they knew it, they were in the book publishing business. Their first collection was called *Home Rhymes*. It was 136 pages, and they printed 800 copies.

Guest was eventually syndicated and was carried by more than 300 newspapers. For more than 30 years, Guest never missed a deadline. His philosophy was his link to success: "I take simple everyday things that happen to me, and I figure it happens to a lot of other people and I make simple rhymes out of them."

10

Pinehurst: The Village

On Thursdays at around 9:05 a.m., Timothy Gold climbs into his restored black 1951 Chevrolet pickup truck with side rails and heads to work. His house is located on course No. 1 at Pinehurst. His trip into town takes him by the stables and barn, Victorian homes and to the corner business district of the village of Pinehurst. The entire drive takes him about five minutes.

Gold often ponders his new life. He smiles and quips, "Let's see, I live five minutes from work, I watch golfers on the fairways…watch a few horses…There is basically no crime. Well, to be honest, it's a touch of spiritual refreshment."

Tim and his wife, Sally, own Burchfield's Golf Gallery. The gallery is a mix of golf memorabilia, photographs, signed pieces and fine art. The store sits on the corner of the business district in the Pinehurst Village.

Gold remembers that not too long ago his mission in life was a little different. "I was selling upscale homes, and my wife was a CPA in Florida," he says remembering the days when his goal was a little different than moving $16,000 watercolors.

Pinehurst was an oasis that took them away from busy professional careers in Florida five years ago. They were both antique dealers and collectors of art pieces by night when they considered the opportunity of buying Burchfields Golf Gallery.

Just prior to the 1999 Ryder Cup at Brookline, the Golds had a customer ask for a bronze statue of Eddie Lowery, the diminutive caddy for Francis Ouimet at the 1913 U.S. Open. Gold said, "The customer wanted it shipped to California. No problem. We got it there in plenty of time." The $30,000 Lowery statue was the hit of the Ryder Cup party. Burchfield's got the assist.

Walking through the gallery provides immediate memories of the 1999 U.S. Open. "Payne Stewart was the fun-loving player who went from bad boy to the prodigal son," says Gold. "He typifies the kind of place where we live. And in many ways he represents Pinehurst."

From the Ben Hogan 1-iron at Merion, to Jack Nicklaus walking across the Swilken Bridge, to Amen Corner, to Tiger Woods at Pebble Beach: Burchfields captures golf's greatest moments—one piece of art at a time.

The Holly Inn

When you say the word "Holly" in the village of Pinehurst, a visitor is usually referencing "a grand lady of elegance." The Holly Inn personifies a landmark of major proportions in Pinehurst. Opened on New Year's Eve in 1895, it was the first building in the village.

The Holly was not the elegant and grand lady in the '80s and early '90s. It had reached a state of functional obsolescence. The Victorian-style inn deserved a refurbishing. In April of 2000, the Holly Inn re-opened its doors following a floor-to-ceiling renovation that returned the classic property to the charmed elegance it claimed when it was opened by founder James Tufts in the early days of the resort.

Pinehurst purchased the property in September of 1997. In January of 1998 the restoration process began.

"The Holly Inn adds another jewel in the crown of Pinehurst," said Patrick Corso, president of Pinehurst. "Guests experience the charm of the 19th century with the finest amenities of the 20th century."

Some of the upgrades include data ports for internet access, valet parking and turndown services, along with videoconferencing capabilities, and most importantly, a bistro-style dining room known as "1895." When the Holly first opened in 1895, it too was state of the art and luxurious. It had electric lights, steam heat and telephones!

Round and Round

Like many things that have been introduced in Pinehurst, there is a European flair, including the oft-used method for diverting busy motorists in the correct direction—the Pinehurst traffic circle. First introduced in the 1950s, the Pinehurst traffic circle is like the Bermuda triangle—some people just never escape. The unwritten motorist rule is to have the intended direction you're heading in mind before you enter the circle, because, once you're in the loop, the signs and the confusion begin.

Europe is known for its traffic circles, where speeding motorists go around and around, searching for the lane and the exit, which allows them to take alternate veins to desired destinations. In 1998, the Pinehurst traffic circle was spinning people into each other, not exactly into their desired route. The traffic accident count was around 145 documented accidents annually, and the U.S. Open was coming to town.

Time to re-evaluate the logistical arteries of the traffic circle.

Built in 1958, the circle was a little unique in that it had five roads (veins) feeding into and out of the circles. It is common for a traffic circle to have four legs, but with five, the visual and the lane changing can get even the most focused driver confused. The circle had not really had a makeover of any amount for nearly 40 years. That was until the traffic count numbers came to the desk of the state department of transportation. Will Garner said he would permit changes of an estimated $900,000. The state took away the inner lane of traffic. "It will be 10 to 12 years before today's traffic delays return," said Gardner.

The result was a 50 percent reduction in accidents. Instead of the many fender benders, the elimination of one lane and the increase in visible signage allowed easy entrance and easy exit from the congestion it previously caused.

"That thing is a joke," said Harvie Ward. "People don't know how to read signs, commit to a direction and exit properly. Some things just need to stay in Scotland and that is one of them."

Ward really doesn't understand the point of the confusing spin-off lanes. The traffic circle just offers another excuse for golfers who are late for tee times.

Maniac Hill

Some call it a proving ground. Others call it a lesson center. The real action at Pinehurst takes place at the factory of Pinehurst—Maniac Hill. Not only was Pinehurst instrumental in the evolution of golf in America, Pinehurst was the birthplace of practice tee sessions. Today it is a hive of activity with buckets of Pinnacles, blisters on hands, grimaces, sweat, words and more balls. Just prior to a recent women's North and South amateur, Maniac Hill was dotted with players with ponytails. An attendant was rapidly filling five-gallon wire baskets of balls with more striped ammunition.

Longtime resident John Derr said, "It really is amazing that Maniac Hill has been on Pinehurst longer than I can remember. When asked who named the driving range, Derr said, "Nobody. It named itself."

Maniac Hill became a teaching area and really another product of the Scottish invasion. The lads from Scotland won the North and South Open in the early years and had the experience in the game. That championship had a major effect on American golf because it attracted the best professionals. The early pros studied each other, exchanging advice and observations. According to writer Herb Graffis, "A fair-sized galley of men who were cheerful givers in the pro-am competitions that sandwiched the North and South

Open with pleasant and proficient hustling of solvent amateurs by impecunious professionals." Bottom line, the money-hungry professionals schooled the wealthy open-eyed amateurs on Maniac Hill to make a buck so they could travel down the road to their next tourney. And it wasn't until 1913, when Tom McNamara won, that there was a bend in the learning curve of golf. And some people who were playing the game at the highest level didn't know how to teach. One early player, Freddie McLeod, said, "The first five years we were pros we should have paid pupils for taking lessons."

Some of the early golfing scholars were names like Snead, Sarazen, and Hogan. Some of their teachers were Scots who wielded the club like a baton. Graffis writes, "Wee Freddie McLeod had the finger and wrist that had him using a couple of woods, 4-irons and a putter changing faces so they'd be like 20 clubs today. Until a few years ago, Freddie would take a 7-iron, which was about a mashie-niblick, and work a ball like he was using a yo-yo. The American lads imitated, adapted, improvised and gradually came out with a style of their own, much of it due to the basic training on Pinehurst's hill."

That is why Tommy Armout said, "Maniac Hill is to golf what Kitty Hawk is to flying." While Orville and Wilbur were busy in 1903 preparing on the sand dunes in Kitty Hawk to fly an estimated 852 feet in 52 seconds, Donald Ross was a couple of hundred miles away winning the North and South Open. Graffis said, "The probability is that some contestant at Pinehurst hit a golf ball longer than a Wright plane traveled its first airborne day."

Donald Ross saw Maniac Hill as a great invention. Learn to swing before going on the course—what a profound ingredient to the growing game. And it was this lesson and the practice tee at Maniac Hill that replaced what in Scotland had become known as the only way to learn, instruction on the course, a playing lesson.

Reg Jones, chief tournament organizer, remembers the tournament committee considering its use just prior to the 1999 U.S. Open. "Nobody said anything about Maniac Hill, because, well, it was Maniac Hill." This will not be the case, however, in 2005. Maniac Hill will be the site of the Corporate Village. The "Hill" will be relocated. "It was a tough decision," said Jones. The driving range for the 2005 U.S. Open will be moved to fairways on the No. 3 and No. 5 courses.

Davis Love III, said, "It's really where I learned to play golf as a junior golfer with my dad at the *Golf Digest* schools."

The best players in the world since the 1900s have made it the launching pad for swing-based education. "Sometimes I think more happens on Maniac Hill than the No. 2 golf course. If you think the No. 2 course beats you up, spend an afternoon on the Hill," Harvie Ward said.

On a certain June day prior to the qualifying for the women's North and South, players dot the practice area, rifling balls into the Carolina air.

Kelly McCall, one of the Pinehurst teaching professionals says there are regulars. "One of the junior members was recently hitting balls during a light rain and lost the grip on his iron. The club ended up on the roof of the Padgett Teaching Center.

From March through November golf schools keep Maniac Hill busy with education. Several members hit balls every day. McCall said, "It is a good environment, we use videotaping, permanent mirrors and have a great short-game area."

Steve Dahl is a local high school athletic director who moonlights at Maniac Hill and knows the routine.

"The best time to hit balls is around 6:00 p.m. A lot of the guests are at dinner and the place is quiet."

The practice facility continues to turn out prodigies with practice. The sign in front of the teaching center says it all:

"The Pinehurst practice range was built in 1913 and dubbed Maniac Hill, one assumes, in honor of all the golf nuts who learned the game of golf here."

Tommy Armour remembers a lesson Phil Perkins gave him: He said, "Tommy, your right knee is stuck." Armour never won the North and South, finishing second in 1928 and 1929.

Maniac Hill was also a venue of an Australian gentleman named Joe Kirkwood. He would do "circus tricks" with the golf ball. Professionals at the North and South Open invited Kirkwood to their clubs for exhibitions, which became another form of golf entertainment. Soon, the Hahns, Jack Redmond and Joe Ezar started hitting the ball from their knees, off elongated tees with rubber hose-shafted clubs—all to the delight of crowds around the country.

Not even Dick Tufts knew who named Maniac Hill. Like most everything at Pinehurst, Maniac Hill is one of the parts that make it a Mecca of American golf.

Tame Squirrels, Rocking Chairs, Chirping Birds

The Carolina Hotel is an understated elegant hotel with knicker-clad bell hops opening doors and saying hello (they claim they wore the knickers long before Payne Stewart made that little putt).

The squirrels don't run for cover, but rather they scamper between feet, tires and white rocking chairs.

And possibly the most memorable sense of Pinehurst is the first impression. No, not turning into the village for the first time or driving up to the Carolina. The Pinehurst operator says, "It's a beautiful day at Pinehusrt."

Wait. It's a beautiful day at Pinehurst?

Ma'am, the sun is nowhere in sight, and it is raining sideways. The pine trees are bending and it looks as though they might snap in two. I just heard a meteorologist say something about the impending lightning and you're saying, "It's a beautiful day at Pinehurst"?

"Sir, it is a statement of attitude."

Now we're getting somewhere. My mother always said nothing is perfect. Well, Pinehurst is perfect in its imperfections. The floors in the Pine Crest and the Manor Inn are not perfectly level. The swimming pool at the Carolina does not have a slide, a kiddy pool or a hot tub. The Tufts Archives do not have every golf book written (I couldn't find *Masters of the Millennium* in their mix).

But the hot maple syrup at the Carolina for breakfast was heated. The crowd on Maniac Hill seemed like they were dancing in the sun. There was a group of senior citizens playing the most formal form of bocce ball I have ever seen in front of the Pinehurst Country Club.

Everything was in its place. The Putter Boy sundial was next to the putting green. The Donald Ross message was next to the starters' shack. The sky was Carolina blue and the pine scent was wafting in the air.

Understated is one way to describe Pinehurst. But there is a real sense that the people who have graced the resort are looking over the place with a spiritual wand.

Is Donald Ross helping Paul Jett steer his Cushman to work on bunkers? Is Dick Tufts telling Reg Jones where to put the corporate village for the 2005 U.S. Open? What really makes me wonder about this place is that some of the people who have walked the fairways, the hallways and the village are among the most well-respected people not only in the game of golf, but in the game of life.

Heritage seems too cheap a word. Tradition does not sound right, either. Pinehurst is a place where the passion of the game surfaces with every made putt.

When I was in the middle of this book project, I stopped by to see a man named Bob Tufts. Tufts is involved with real estate at the Mid-South Club, but he is as much behind the progression of Pinehurst as any other single individual. His family wanted it that way.

He asked me if I had a minute to see a sequence on his laptop computer.

What I saw next revealed what every golfing expert, novice, beginner, hacker will feel over the next year. Tufts showed me slow-motion footage of Payne Stewart lining up his putt on the 72nd hole. I was transfixed; I knew the ball curled in the hole. I knew that he was going to strike a pose, hug his caddy and then shake Mickelson's hand. I knew all that. And still. The chills ran up my spine like a spider taking a stroll.

Legend of Waddy Stokes/Forest Who?

Ken Venturi opened his broadcast of the 1979 San Diego Open with a unique look at the new tour statistical categories: Greens in regulation, putting average, driving distance, eagle leaders, birdie leaders, and then he got to the most important category—scoring average. Venturi looked at the name of the player leading the category and did a double take. "Waddy Stokes, 70.0." Venturi said, "I don't know who Waddy Stokes is, but he sure is beating the hell out of Tom Watson."

Stokes, who played on the PGA Tour from 1978-80, had actually played in just one tournament prior to the new statistical categories being released. Stokes remembers, " I played the week before and shot 70 in the opening round. I shot 83 on day two and missed the cut, but I signed the scorecard in the wrong place. I was DQ'd and instead of counting both scores, they just counted my 70. Here I was leading the stroke average."

Today, Stokes is the resident professional at the most up-and-coming private course in Pinehurst, Forest Creek. Stokes has had a relationship with Tom Fazio, Forest Creek's designer on several new courses in the south, including Western Carolina's Wade Hampton. Stokes said Fazio was given a piece of property and told by the ownership that they wanted a really good golf course. The result is a spectacular layout, just over 7,100 yards from the long tees. "We are known for our hard, fast greens, kind of like [Oakmont, Pine Valley Augusta National] from a greens standpoint. Here quality shots get quality results, and bad shots get bad results. But our course is not as penal as Pine Valley."

The most intriguing aspect of Forest Creek is the "hog hole." The ownership wanted to complete the round with a long beat-all-end-all par five over water with a 170-yard carry on the third shot. Fazio said they couldn't build a hole where the majority of the players were going to plunk a ball in the water, add them up and then head to the parking lot with a frown.

"What he ended up doing was building a really great par four and then the 'hog hole,'" Stokes said. The hog hole ends up being the Forest Creek 19th hole. It is called the "hog hole" because you can lose on the first 18 and then "bet the whole hog on the last"—a par three over the pond. Stokes says all bets are usually settled here.

The membership includes original member Harvie Ward, who still does some teaching, and Michael Jordan, who according to Stokes, "Likes to get on the course and play round and round."

Ward recently played a round with a 10-handicapper from Chapel Hill. On the 10th hole, the player looked around and said, "Where is everybody? There is nobody here." The player happened to be a former basketball coach from the University of North Carolina named Smith.

Bill Reichart, a former Olympic Hockey player for the U.S. team in 1976, is one of the more than 750 members at Forest Creek. He has a typical hockey player's build, is stout, and he hits the ball with a slap shot-type, flat-swing plane. He shot 68 on his 68th birthday.

"Only one moment in time could that occur," Stokes said.

One moment in time seems to be a theme that runs throughout the Pinehurst community.

Michael Jordan

Henry Caldwell rarely plays golf at Forest Creek. It is usually the result of a boyhood friend's invitation. Henry Caldwell never breaks par at Forest Creek. Caldwell is never on the fairway at Forest Creek. An average player, Caldwell tracked down his errant tee ball in early spring of 2002, but found another ball, belonging to Michael Jordan. Stamped on the ball was a swoosh and an MJ/23. Must be from that 7-handicap player from Chapel Hill, via the Chicago Bulls and Washington Wizards and now in the oblivion of the unemployed. Not a bad keepsake for a round of golf that by Caldwell's standard was very unspectacular.

Jordan's golf legacy is not as impressive as his basketball legacy, of course. But, like any true aficionado, he searches for the diamonds to play as he says, "with his golf buddies."

In 1988, he had just won the Most Valuable Player Award. The Detroit Pistons again bumped the Bulls from the playoffs. Where was Michael Jordan? He was at Pinehurst playing 36 holes a day. Training camp? He had a 7:30 a.m. lesson followed by his first 18. An hour practice session, lunch, another hour of practice and his second 18. This went on for two weeks. His favorite course was probably the Rees Jones favorite, Pinehurst No. 7.

A repeat performance? The day the season ended, the Chicago Bulls star headed 800 miles Southeast to Pinehurst. He left Chicago around 5:00 a.m. He was on the first tee for his 10 a.m. tee time.

Davis Love walked into Carmichael Gymnasium in 1984 and asked M.J., "Do you want to play some golf?" He says he feels like "I gave Dillinger his first gun."

Jordan rarely makes it over to No. 2 these days. He prefers a more discreet refuge at Forest Creek.

Donna Andrews

When Andrews escapes the fairways of the LPGA Tour, she can often be found down on a farm near Pinehurst. It's interesting that both in the sport of golf and in the case of dressage, which she enjoys with her Hanoverian mare, grace and power are harnessed for the right time.

Back in 1998, the former Tar Heel was standing 107 yards from the flagstick on the sixth hole in the final round of the LPGA's Long Drugs Challenge. To this point, her 1998 season was uneventful. There was a respectable fifth-place finish in the Nabisco Dinah Shore the week prior, an event she won in 1993. But as her wedge shot went air borne and then nestled in the four and a half inch hole in the earth for an eagle, in the span of eight seconds her cerebral game was ignited. Andrews fought off bogeys on the back nine in Lincoln, California, and went on to beat Sweden's Carin Koch for her sixth LPGA Tour win. The win was a catalyst for an impressive tournament run in 1998, a run rivaled only by players named Se Ri Pak and Annika Sorenstam. After a tie for sixth at the Mercury Titleholders Championship, Andrews finished second four straight times, including the McDonald's LPGA Championship. At the Sara Lee Classic in Nashville, she enjoyed the local sounds of Vince Gill and Neil McCoy enough to shoot 205 and finish tied with Barb Mucha, Jenny Lidback, and Nancy Lopez. Although Mucha won the tournament on the second play-off hole, Andrews kept up her pace on Tour.

And it might not have been all golf that led Andrews to become the leading money winner on Tour in June. "After my win I flew the red-eye flight home and on that next day, we had a little baby colt born on our farm," said Andrews. She even claimed that the week tending to the new colt was so exhausting that getting back to the Tour grind would be like a vacation.

Andrews continues to battle each week on the LPGA Tour. And as she continues to put her soft spike stamp on the LPGA tour, the former Tar Heel may want to eventually retire to the Pinehurst farm to become a full-time horse whisperer.

11

The Caddies

Jeff Ferguson

"The No. 2 course is all about missing the green in the right places," said Jeff Ferguson, 2001 inductee in the Pinehurst Caddy Hall of Fame.

It was 1983 and the rock band Ratt was starting to gain acceptance with a lot of Southern rockers. Among the followers was a young man named Jeff Ferguson.

Ferguson had a Ratt t-shirt he would wear around the *Golf Digest* schools in the summer, waiting for a chance to get a loop. One of the junior golfers he met was Davis Love III. The Love family made Pinehurst a home away from home. Love got to know a friendly caddy, Ferguson, who was just a few years older.

"David and his family spent a lot of time around Pinehurst. Before long, I began to follow Davis at Carolina and I was fortunate to caddy for him in the North and South [which Love won in 1983]." And it was Love, and then a Wake Forest player, Billy Andrade, who gave Ferguson his nickname "Ratman."

Ferguson knows the No. 2 course better than any other caddy walking the fairways. He is already a member of the Pinehurst Caddy Hall of Fame.

Ferguson started caddying at Pinehurst in 1977. "I remember the course when Diamondhead decided they were going to change how it was played. I remember the Love Grass that they put in bunkers. You couldn't get it out of the bunker if you had a clump of that stuff in front of you."

Ferguson has caddied for the likes of Michael Jordan, women's amateur sensation Aree Song (2003 Women's North and South) and in the 1999 U.S. Open for E.J. Pfister.

"Pinehurst is all about hitting the greens in the right spot. It has taken me years to understand the subtle aspects of the golf course. When it gets right down to it, this is a target golf course. There is no trouble off the tees with most players. And length. Just look at some of the junior players these days and how far they hit it," Ferguson says.

Ratman has also seen his share of amateur players drop a ball on the 18th hole at Pinehurst No. 2 to hit "Payne's putt."

Not a Good Walk Spoiled

Mark Twain may have uttered, "Golf is a good walk spoiled," but that really does not apply to Pinehurst. You have not really played Pinehurst until you've walked Pinehurst. Donald Ross did not have golf carts in mind when he laid out the Pinehurst designs. And walking Pinehurst was exactly how Ross configured the holes. After all, Ross was a caddy himself in 1890 in Dornoch, Scotland, when he had to walk the course holding the players' clubs loosely. About this same time, the golf bag (an awkward suitcase style) was invented, which aided the caddies' endeavors. Early on, the bag more resembled Samsonite luggage than something that was designed to hold hickory shafts. Ross understood there was no better way to fully understand the nuances of the course than to have a caddy by your side with a bag. Sure, early on, there were some problems. For some of the best courses in America, providing the service of a caddy is a lost art. Not at Pinehurst.

In 2001, the club began to recognize the history of loopers at Pinehurst by inducting several caddies (past and present) into a celebrated circle. Their integral part of golf at Pinehurst spans generations. The Pinehurst Caddie Hall of Fame includes: John T. Daniel, Barry Google, Jeff Ferguson, Fletcher Gaines, Teddy Marley, Willie McRae, Robert Robinson, Hilton Rodgers, Robert Stafford, Jimmy Steed and caddy master Jack Williams.

Fletcher Gaines might be best known as the caddy for Curtis Strange from 1975-76. Strange said, "I for one know that it was you and I as a team that brought out the best in each of us. You are a wonderful caddy, but a better person." Gaines retired in 1995 after 57 years of service.

Robert Robinson, nicknamed "Hardrock," was noted for his tap-dancing ability—not on the greens, but in the caddy area and on the dance floor.

Then there was Hilton Rodgers, better known as the "Doctor." Rodgers was known for his great memory and the ability to recite the yardages on the sprinkler heads from inside the clubhouse. He also had the uncanny ability to tell the slope of the putt when placement on the green was indicated.

Willie McRae started caddying at Pinehurst in 1943. He toted Fred Daley's bag in 1951 and was on the winning bag for 1970 North and South champion, Gary Cowan. McRae's cousin, Charlie McRae, also caddies at Pinehurst. "One of the old-timers," McRae remembers the day he caddied for Beth Daniel in the North and South Amateur. "I'll never forget her father telling me, 'She's kind of hot-headed, but I want you to know that I expect her to do whatever you want her to do.'" McRae reveals several course secrets for amateur players.

For Harvie Ward, Barney Google was at his side in his historic win at the 1948 North and South. Davis Love III had Jeff Ferguson in the 1983 North and South. Ferguson, 45, the youngest in the Caddie Hall of Fame, has toted the bag for Women's North and South winners Beth Bauer and Candy Hannemann. Ferguson was the caddy for Aree Song in the 2003 event until she withdrew due to injury.

In 1911, a photographer assembled a group of more than 150 men and boys who worked as caddies at Pinehurst. The effort was preserved in a scrapbook called, "Faces of Taylortown." Taylortown, located next to Pinehurst, is a town where a lot of the caddies lived.

The game of golf was not meant to have gas or electric carts as chariots of transportation. At Pinehurst, golf is celebrated as a walking sport, and caddies are part of the continuing traditions of the game.

12

The LPGA
at Pinehurst

Peggy Kirk Bell

In the early 1950s, Babe Zaharias and Peggy Kirk Bell knew that women's golf was only going to get rolling with a little self-promotion. At the Western Open, the press was hungry for news on the fledging state of the women's game. And so Babe Zaharias quenched their thirst. Just when Babe and Kirk had their attention, a plot was hatched. The Babe whispered to Kirk, "You know something, we've got to get a Women's Open started." Knowing full well the press perceived the importance of an event based on the purse money (which in those days was between $1,500 and $2,000), the Babe said to Kirk, "We are going to tell the press there is a $10,000 Women's Open on the horizon." Bell's reply was, "You know we can't afford to do that." Babe retorted, "Yeah, but we are just not going to pay anyone." So the press, eager for information, sat and listened to the Babe announce that there would be a new movement, a U.S. Women's Open. That statement started the ball rolling. Peggy Kirk Bell said, "She was one of the best promoters of our game." During this same time, the Babe played a practice round for the Women's Western Open. When she finished, the press would be vigilant about her score. She would disclose she shot a 70. Kirk remembers playing with the Babe for this fabulous practice round. "I would tell her, 'What are you talking about? You didn't shoot a 70 today, more like a 78.'" The Babe's response was emphatic. "They don't want to hear I shot a 78 today. I'm going to tell them what they want to hear." The article in the paper the following morning was Babe warms up with a 70 in the practice round for Western Open.

And even though the truth did not exactly rise to the top in the early days of the LPGA, what has happened to women's golf is much of what the Babe espoused in 1952. Only Kirk Bell is now one of the loudest voices.

When you say Ma Bell in golf circles, most people have a story or two. Born in Findlay, Ohio, she learned the game as a teenager. Her amateur career hit a high note when she helped the U.S. soundly defeat Great Britain/Ireland seven and one half to one and one half in 1950.

She then helped form the LPGA with such players as the Babe, Patty Berg and Louise Suggs. Back then, they offered $150,000 in prize money for 21 events starting in 1952. In 1953, Peggy, along with her husband, Warren, purchased the Pine Needles resort. She played on the LPGA for more than a decade, but soon settled down with her husband to raise three children. She helped build the women's game the same way Donald Ross built golf courses. She was a pioneer, but most importantly she was a spokesperson for the advent of women to the growing sport. Still active in the management of both Pine Needles and Mid-Pines resorts, the USGA came knocking again in the 1990s and she obliged, being the honorary chairman for the 1996 U.S. Women's Open, which returned again in 2001. "We started small. We hosted a Girl's Junior Championship in 1989, and then in 1991 we hosted the Women's USGA Senior Amateur Championship. And then, I said, now if we'd just had the Open, we'd have it covered." The Open arrived in Peggy Kirk Bell's back yard in 1996, and it returned in 2001. The purse for the 1996 Open was $1.2 million.

In 1996, Peggy Kirk Bell reflected on the women who have paraded to her remote corner of the world since 1989. Brandie Burton and Vickie Goetze were junior players when Pine Needles hosted the Girl's Junior Championship. There was a player who stayed with Peggy Kirk Bell in the early '90s who played golf at Arizona. "She came in and I had an awful time with her name. I said, 'You need a name like Jane or Anne. I just can't remember your name.' I kept calling her Heineken." In 1995, when Annika Sorenstam walked off a different Donald Ross layout to win the U.S. Open, Kirk Bell was standing there to congratulate her. "Heineken, now you've won a big one." Heineken won again in 1996, this time at Ma Bell's course.

13

The U.S. Amateur

Captain Sutton

In 1980, Ronald Reagan was president, and Mount St. Helens was spewing steam and ash.

On the fairways of the Country Club of North Carolina and the No. 2 course in Pinehurst, Fred Couples was the story. The Seattle native toured the Country Club of North Carolina and Pinehurst No. 2. He received medallist honors and the University of Houston All-American was a good bet to make a run in match play. Mark O'Meara was defending his title from 1979 when he beat John Cook in Cleveland at Canterbury Country Club. Couples and O'Meara had company, the reigning North and South Champion, Hal Sutton. He was a 22-year-old from the bayou who was steering a golf ball considerably well.

Sutton was paired in the finals of the U.S. Amateur against Bob Lewis Jr. of Warren, Ohio. Lewis was the oldest player at the time to reach the finals since the matches went to match-play in 1973. Sutton managed to play the outward nine in one under for a two-hole lead. He managed to win three more holes to extend his lead to five-up before lunch.

Lewis never won another hole. Sutton won on the 10th hole when both players parred. Sutton was on a 109 match-hole stretch in which he played 13-under par. Lewis was two-over par over a stretch of 108 holes. Sutton earned the Havemeyer Trophy.

Harvie Ward

E. Harvie Ward Jr. was a champion. He was a champion because he didn't really care for second place. He was a champion because he paid his dues on the range and competed on the fairways.

Fresh out of the service, Harvie Ward, 20, wanted to play on a national stage, the big one, the U.S. Amateur, but his dad said, "No way, you're not ready for the national amateur." And so, he went off to school at the University of North Carolina in September of 1946.

He worked on his golf game enough over the next year to convince his dad his game was ready for the next level. On his plane flight out to Pebble Beach for the 1947 U.S. Amateur, he sat next to a nice man from Augusta, Georgia, Cliff Roberts. Ward remembers Roberts saying, "Well, young man, I am chairman of the Masters." Not overly impressed, Ward listened on. "If you make it to the quarterfinals, you'll get an automatic invitation to my tournament." Ward said he didn't know too much about the Masters, but he was determined to get an invitation. He made it to the quarterfinals. "Sure enough, lo and behold, Cliff Roberts sent me my first invitation to the 1948 Masters," Ward said.

Ward showed up on Magnolia Lane in what one Augusta member described as a beat-up jalopy with "Augusta or bust" printed on the side. Ward would like to set the record straight, "It did have 'Augusta or bust' on the side, but it was not a beat-up car. It was a tan Ford convertible. I drove in, and the doorman said, 'With all that you've got all over your car, you'll have to park over here in the employee parking lot.' Hell, I didn't care, it was a place to park." Ward's trip yielded a 51st-place finish in his first Masters. He would be back nine more times, but the tan Ford convertible never returned.

Determined to improve his game, he headed back to UNC. He wanted to show he belonged.

There was no way a sophomore from the University of North Carolina was going to leave his Zeta Psi frat house to compete in one of the most prestigious amateur golf events and do well. The story of Ward at the 1948 North South is well documented. He beat Arnold Palmer in the semifinals. "Arnold was not new to me. Back in those days, all the matches we played in college were match play. So I had seen Arnold before and he knew me," said Ward. Ward finished off Palmer five and four in order to face the heir to the Champion spark plug empire, Frank Stranahan.

This was very similar to the 1936 PGA Championship at Pinehurst. Here was a weight-lifting, dark-complected Adonis, and a kid who left the baby blue university just to test his game.

What a lot of people did not calculate was that as Ward kept winning matches and getting close to the weekend, there was a groundswell back in Chapel Hill. "They had classes, and I was just going along winning the match. When they showed up on Saturday, it was embarrassing. You would have thought it was a football game instead of a golf tournament. Guys and girls were running around barefooted. Frank had his mother, dad and his sister. And I had 2,000 students pulling for me. Every time I made a shot they'd cheer, and every time Frank would miss a shot, they'd cheer. At that time, the proper Pinehurst people came out and had coats and ties, and they were very elegant people. You know, they stood around with their heads high and their noses up. They must have thought, 'What has Pinehurst come to?' But the kids didn't know any better. They didn't mean anything by it. They were just pulling for me." He adds, "It was like a team environment, only it was just me against Frank." Ward was carried off the course by the Chapel Hill throng in bow ties and dresses, the same way Frances Ouimet left Brookline after beating Vardon and Ray in the U.S. Open in 1913.

As Ward looked back on that week, he does have one regret. He said years later he felt like he contributed to the death of Donald Ross that week. Ross died of a heart attack during the week of the 1948 North South. "I know I didn't kill him, but we did make some noise that week," he said.

Ward won the event, and then lost to Stranahan in the finals in 1949. "You know Harvie, you should have won this year and I should have won in '48," said Stranahan.

Donald Ross

By 1955, Ward was playing in his ninth straight U.S. Amateur in Richmond, Virginia at the Country Club of Virginia. He was playing just a few hours away from where he went to prep school in Lynchburg, Virginia (Virginia Episcopal School). The obstacle for Ward in the matches was his first-round match. He played Ray Palmer from Illinois. He was one-down going to the 18th hole. The hole had been changed to a par four, with a cross-bunker coming into play just prior to the green. As both players approached their drives, they knew one player, whose ball was a mere eight inches in the rough, was not going to be able to carry the cross bunker with a good chance to make par. "I had been to the Amateur nine times, and as I walked up to the balls back in that first match I remember saying, 'Don't tell me I am going to come within eight inches of having another chance to win,'" Ward said. It was determined that Palmer received the misfortune of having to play out of the rough. He had to lay up short of the cross-bunker and ended up making bogey. Ward made par to extend the match to extra holes. He won the match with a 15-foot birdie putt in the 19th. Ward ended up beating William Hydmann in the finals, 9 and 8. "I shot 66 in the first 18 and just blistered the golf course," Ward said.

A year later Ward beat Chuck Kocsis at Knollwood Country Club, five and four. This time he had to come from behind, playing the final 13 holes in five under par. He became the sixth back-to-back champion, but it had been 21 years since the feat had been accomplished.

Ward eventually played in 10 Masters tournaments. At age 31, he finished fourth in 1957 when Doug Ford came up to him on the last hole and told him: "If I make six I lose, if I make five I tie, and if I make four I win." Ford ended up holing his bunker shot for the win.

A native of Tarboro, NC, Ward, 77, currently plays to a four-handicap at Forest Creek Golf Club in Pinehurst. He gives lessons selectively and remembers being chided about not ever turning professional. His sentiment is understandable: "Why play professional golf in the 1950s when you had to beat Jimmy Demaret, Ben Hogan, and Sam Snead to win $26,000? I would certainly have turned pro in a heartbeat, if they were making the kind of money they are making now. But I was making more money doing what I was doing." Back then Toski was the leading money winner at something like $49,000.

Times have changed.

Goetze vs. Burton: 1989 U.S. Women's Amateur

Shute vs. Thomson, Ward vs. Stranahan, Inman vs. Love III. These were all great Pinehurst matches, but when it comes to the best matches to ever be played at Pinehurst, one interesting match involved two players from different sides of the golfing fence who met regularly on the junior and women's amateur scene. They now meet regularly on the LPGA Tour.

Vickie Goetze (now Vickie Goetze Ackerman) and Brandie Burton met at the 1989 U.S. Women's Amateur at Pinehurst No. 2. Burton, a native of Rialto, California, was the West coast power to Goetze's East coast finesse. This was the start of the differences between these two rising players.

Goetze grew up in Hull, Georgia, where life is simple. Her father, Gregg, a high school psychologist, toted Goetze's bag for the amateur competition. Her brother Nicky was runner-up to Brian Montgomery in the 1986 U.S. Junior. Vickie was a softspoken player who had a straight game and a magician's ability around the greens.

Burton was the Joanne Carner of the junior and amateur scene. Her stealth-like glare often intimidates her partners, and long, missile-like drives were her trademark.

Burton would attempt to reach par fives in two. Goetze would sink two-shots with precision and then drop a pin-seeking iron shot at her opponent. Grace vs. power.

In 1989, Goetze was 16 years old. She weighed all of 110 pounds and talked just above a whisper. Burton, 17, was coming off a 1-up defeat of Goetze just down the road in Southern Pines at the U.S. Girl's Junior at Pine Needles Lodge. Revenge was Goetze's order of business. They had been in similar battles for the past three years on the junior circuit. Burton knew Goetze had the mental make up to withstand her distance advantage off the tee.

Burton opened up at Pinehurst No. 2 with par at the 392-yard second hole. Goetze hit two metal woods and was still short of the green. Burton won the second, birdied the short par-four third and the par-five fifth. In the span of four holes, Burton was three-up.

But, as in match play, anything can happen. And with Goetze in the greenside bunker on the fifth, Burton had designs on moving to four-up. This is when the magical qualities of the Goetze short game started to shine. She played a sand shot to within 20 feet and made the putt. Burton struggled to get down from just off the green. Goetze said later, "That swing in the match gave me some momentum."

Goetze played solid golf on the back nine, winning five holes to Burton's one, leaving Goetze with a two-up lead at lunch. Goetze picked up one more hole on the front nine, escaping her poor early-morning start. However, Goetze stumbled on the backside with bogeys at the 10th and 11th. Burton managed pars and pulled within one hole of her counterpart.

With the momentum on her side, Burton sent one of her tee missiles off-line, leaving Goetze to regain a two-up lead. She won the 14th, and the stage was set for Goetze to play conservative and slowly finish off her opponent. But at the par-three 15th, Goetze took a 5-wood and placed her ball 30 feet from the hole. When her putt suprisingly found the bottom of the cup, she completed her comeback with a 4 and 3 win.

Goetze was three down after four holes and ended up winning 4 and 3.

"That was the best I played. But I lost to birdies and that's the way you should lose," said Burton.

Goetze would win the 1992 U.S. Amateur and NCAA Championship before turning professional in 1993. Burton, after attending Arizona State for one year, qualified for the LPGA Tour at the end of the 1990 season.

When the dust settles from the last century of women's amateur competition, Brandie Burton and Vickie Goetze will be remembered for different games, but the same competitive spirit.

1936 PGA

The *Raleigh News and Observer* documented the showdown in November of 1936 between two contrasting characters in the PGA Championship—H. Densmore "Denny" Shute and Jimmy Thomson.

Bob Cavagnaro wrote, "James Wilfred Stevenson Thomson, the blasting blond giant with the terra-cotta complexion, and Densmore Shute, who has a contrastingly ashen appearance, today shot their way into the finals of the Professional Golfer's Association championship.

"With styles as different as their appearances—Thompson the acknowledged longest hitter in the game and Shute, on the short side of the tees but one of the deadliest players about the greens—staged remarkable Horatio Alger comebacks to have a chance at the crown relinquished earlier in the week by Johnny Revolta of Chicago."

Thomson rallied to beat Craig Wood four and three. Shute, having stretches of what Cavagnaro called "hot and cold golf," came from two-down with five to play—and beat—"Wild" Billy Behlhorn, 1-up.

Thomson was the Goliath to Shute's David. Thomson outdrove Shute by 60 yards on some holes, but Shute, a 32-year-old Brae Burn Country Club pro used guile and a steady short game to beat the long-hitting Thomson. With the win,

Shute earned $1,000 and a spot on the 1937 Ryder Cup team. Cavagnaro noted, "While he beat Thomson with his steady short game, Shute, strangely enough, put a crusher on with a surprising display of power on the par-five 473-yard 34th, where the match ended. Jimmy sliced a 270-yard tee shot into the woods, planted his second in the bunker near the green and exploded 15 feet short of the cup and putted past.

Shute meantime cracked a 240-yard drive, his longest of the windy day. He followed it up with a spanking spoon shot that traveled as far and stopped less than five feet from the cup. After Thomson failed to get up and down from 15 feet, he knocked Shute's ball away, conceding the putt and an eagle. And shook his conqueror's hand.

Opinions varied for Shute's success. The 32 year old gave up considerable size and power to Thomson. He just got the ball in the hole in fewer strokes.

The field for the 1936 PGA was impressive. Walter Hagen failed to make match play by one stroke. Noted players Bill Burke, Craig Wood, Gene Sarazen, defending champ Revolta and Henry Picard were among those who qualified at 147 or better to make match play. Others making match play included Jimmy Demaret, Horton Smith, Paul Runyan and Tommy Armour.

History of Championship Golf

It was Hal Sutton's turn to talk on Saturday night before the Sunday singles matches at the Ryder Cup at Brookline in 1999. Sutton has a husky Bayou twang that reverberated through the room: "I believe there is more talent on the sixth floor than there is on the fifth, but we have to play with more emotion. We've got to raise our fists and get the crowd into it."

Everyone knows what happened next. America's team created more of a stir in Boston than the tea party.

Sutton backed up his bayou beckon with a four and two win over Darren Clarke. He added passion on the last day. He called the week in Boston one of the lowest and highest points of his golfing career.

In 2004, Sutton will captain team U.S.A. to Oakland Hills. The Detroit crowd is one of the most boisterous on the PGA Tour. Now there is a sense of urgency and a renewed sense of patriotism to retrieve the Cup in a town that has a penchant for over-celebrations. It is a Donald Ross venue—a place Sutton said has the aura.

And if Sutton, the 1980 U.S. Amateur champion in Pinehurst has something to add as a main ingredient to securing the Cup—it's passion. This ingredient has been with the Europeans—as their main ingredient since St. Andrews.

Have the fairways in America been too green? Is the money driving players away from the pillars of the sport?

Sutton knows Pinehurst principles start with one theme, one ambition when it comes to golf. And his plea to his team in Detroit should sound like something that started in Pinehurst.

This isn't about money, and if you think it is, you simply don't get it. This was first and foremost an amateur game. Foursomes, Four-Ball and match-play make up the foundation of the game as an amateur sport.

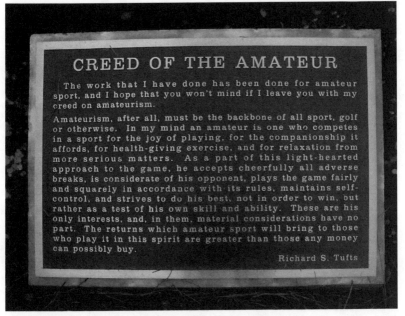

CREED OF THE AMATEUR

The work that I have done has been done for amateur sport, and I hope that you won't mind if I leave you with my creed on amateurism.

Amateurism, after all, must be the backbone of all sport, golf or otherwise. In my mind an amateur is one who competes in a sport for the joy of playing, for the companionship it affords, for health-giving exercise, and for relaxation from more serious matters. As a part of this light-hearted approach to the game, he accepts cheerfully all adverse breaks, is considerate of his opponent, plays the game fairly and squarely in accordance with its rules, maintains self-control, and strives to do his best, not in order to win, but rather as a test of his own skill and ability. These are his only interests, and, in them, material considerations have no part. The returns which amateur sport will bring to those who play it in this spirit are greater than those any money can possibly buy.

Richard S. Tufts

Richard Tufts's legacy is capsulized by this creed.

Pinehurst did not invent amateurism. Pinehurst adopted amateurism because of a man named Richard Tufts. Pinehurst and Tufts grew up together. And it was a singular creed by Tufts that echoes the message that Sutton should pass along. Tufts prefaced his creed:

"The work that I have done has been done for amateur sport, and I hope that you won't mind if I leave you with my creed on amateurism.

"Amateurism, after all, must be the backbone of all sport, golf or otherwise. In my mind an amateur is one who competes in a sport for the joy of playing, for the companionship it affords, for health-giving exercise, and for relaxation for more serious matters. As a part of this light-hearted approach to the game, he accepts cheerfully all adverse

(Left to right) Richard S. Tufts, Donald J. Ross, I.C. Sledge.

breaks, is considerate of his opponent, plays the game fairly and squarely in accordance with its rules, maintains self-control, and strives to do his best, not in order to win, but rather as a test of his own skill and ability. These are his only interests, and, in them, material considerations have no part. The returns which amateur sport will bring those who play it in this spirit are greater than those any money can possibly buy."

And the genre of competitive golf today is best summarized by golf scribe Herbert Warren Wind, "Today, there is so much money at stake in golf tournaments that it overpowers all other considerations. It is a rare player now who seems to enjoy his sport and to regard it as something more than a means to an end."

Pinehurst is about the history of championship golf and the retrieving of some of the fundamental aspects of a changing game. It has a history of brilliant golf from the 1936 PGA Championship between Denny Shute and Jimmy Thomson, to George Dunlap's historic run of North and South Championships, to the 1951 Ryder Cup. Pinehurst might be just over a century old, but it has been home to some of the greatest championships: 1936 PGA, 1951 Ryder Cup, 1962 U.S. Amateur, 1980 U.S. Amateur, 1989 U.S. Women's Amateur, 1994 U.S. Senior Open,1999 U.S. Open, 2005 U.S. Open, 2007 U.S. Amateur.

Recent USGA Bob Jones Award winner Barbara McIntire said, "There was just something special about winning at Pinehurst."

Ray Floyd

"Over a four-day tournament you will play every shot you know how to play. And to me that is the game of golf," Ray Floyd said of Pinehurst.

He was born at Fort Bragg, some say a 3-wood from Pinehurst, and he grew up in nearby Fayetteville, North Carolina. When he returned to play the U.S. Senior Open in 1994, he had been playing competitive golf around the world for 32 years.

"I don't think anybody can take Pinehurst out of their top five, of all the courses around the world. It is a marvelous traditional golf course— a true masterpiece in a natural setting. The greens allow all kinds of shots from around them. It is not a one-dimensional course. And you must think your way around the course."

Floyd knows course design, and he also knows the heritage of the area of Pinehurst. He said prior to the 1994 U.S. Senior Open, "Can you imagine when this course was built? You had hand labor and horse and drag. So the bunkers were carved to use earth to form the green and the slight swells in front to form green subtleties. In a lot of cases the greens appear elevated, but they aren't. They have movement, but it is all natural, which affords you so many opportunities to play golf shots. The skills that you develop as a professional are ones that you use at Pinehurst. And you can appreciate those on a golf course like this because you can literally use all of them here. It is not a 60-degree sand wedge if you miss a green…It is not a bump-and-run if you miss a green. It is not a putt from off the green. It is not a bump into the wall and let it kick up. It is all of those. You can use any of those shots from off the green if you elect. That is tradition, and that is traditional architecture," Floyd said.

That is Pinehurst.

"Great is the art of beginning, but greater the art is of ending."
—*Henry Wadsworth Longfellow*

14

The PGA Tour

In 1935 Donald Ross was getting grass to grow on the Pinehurst greens, and the PGA Tour was in its infancy. In January the PGA announced a total purse of $134,700— for the year! It did not take long for the PGA Tour to find an event for Pinehurst. In 1936 Pinehurst hosted the PGA Championship.

Since 1935, the PGA Tour has recognized Pinehurst as a golfing venue, but it can be argued that the amateur game was more mainstream in the Carolina consciousness before 1950. In the first 50 years of the century, the amateur and professional circuits were both gaining identities and the governing bodies of the sport were setting out to define boundaries. Since the birth of the sport, separating the professional circuit from the amateur was as troublesome to the governing bodies as it was to Ross and Dick Tufts. Bill Campbell insists, "There was not a clearly defined set of boundaries for both amateur and professional play. This would be developed in the latter part of the century." Campbell was part of the team that grappled with the rules of golf and the doctrines regarding "amateur status."

But, like so many PGA Tour and LPGA players today, their memories of their amateur days of Pinehurst are vivid.

Current PGA Tour player Pat Perez finally made it to golf's defining level after turning professional in 1997. In his rookie season (2002), Perez finished 40th on the money list. Jonathan Byrd edged him for Rookie of the Year honors.

Like so many on the PGA Tour, Pinehurst has been part of Perez's amateur past. Perez showed up at Pinehurst in 1993 after dusting Tiger Woods at Torrey Pines to win the Junior World title and claimed the Maxfli PGA Junior. At the age of 17, he developed the confidence that eventually allowed him to earn medalist honors at the PGA Tour Qualifying School in 2001.

Tiger Woods was a similar prodigy who recognized golf's traditional havens in his rise on the PGA Tour. "I first played here in 1992, and it's changed a lot since then. But it is still one of my favorite traditional golf courses. To me, it's one of the ultimate challenges. I don't know why. I think because it's not artificial. When Ross built Pinehurst, they did not have the equipment, so they had to go ahead and use the natural terrain to their advantage. You look at a flat piece of desert like at Arizona State, where they make mounds and valleys where you can't even see. That's what they can now do with our modern equipment. But, I like (Pinehurst) mostly because of the importance of your imagination, especially around the greens."

Woods was a couple of strokes from becoming a factor in the Stewart-Mickelson duel in 1999. From the time he first visited Pinehurst in 1992 to play No. 7, Woods has toured the Pinehurst links with an unconventional short game. Three woods, flop shots, putters, whatever it calls for to feed the ball to crowns on the convex moss.

When Colin Montgomerie showed up for the U.S. Open in 1999 he scratched his head and grimaced as he is accustomed to doing and said, "My caddy is quite funny, he said in our practice round "middle of the green is okay." But, Montgomerie was quick to point out, "He said that 18 straight times today." He adds, "The runoffs on No. 2 are quite similar to Augusta. This has the odd upturned saucer green. You play the 2nd and 5th hole, consider the par 3s at Dornoch and you see that they've copied that." Since Montgomerie is a native Scot, winning on a Ross-designed layout might be extra motivation. "There's a lot of good courses around the world designed by Scots. There's not many that aren't."

And since the U.S. Open has had a European dry spell since Tony Jacklin in 1970, should a European player not break the jinx in 2003, the Pinehurst experience in 2005 might have familiar questions before they tee off on Thursday. This course is particularly suited to the European players. Could this be the week one wins?

In 1999 Great Britain's Lee Westwood answered the same question emphatically. He said, "You have to have a good imagination around the green, be very accurate with the irons, not so accurate as I'd like with the driver and it doesn't matter that the course suits Europeans. It comes down to the best player will win."

The LPGA's Brandie Burton won the North and South in 1990. She then showed up in contention at the 1996

U.S. Open at Pine Needles. "This place is special to me. I find a way to relax and play my best golf. It is partly due to the fact that I like Ross's design work. I don't know, I have always played well here." Just before Burton left the interview tent in 1996 she was asked how she would relax before the final round.

"I think I'll just throw a line in Lake Pinehurst and see what happens." Annika Sorenstam won the U.S. Open in 1996 going away, but Burton never lost the inspiration to play her best golf at Pinehurst.

"It is hard to describe. This place will always be special to me."

Proving ground? Pinehurst has a spirit in the sandy soil that grabs hold of some of the finest young players in the game. It seems to usher them to other worldwide golfing venues. Some achieve a great deal of success. Others are humbled by the game's exactness and evasive characteristics.

But they somehow always return to Pinehurst.

Epilogue

Donald Ross often said golf and sand go together. He believed that sand lent itself to the sculpture of golf courses on Scottish links. In Pinehurst, Ross used this combination to sculpt an arena that has withstood the test of time better than any sporting venue in America. From 1895, the little town known as Pinehurst started to grow muscles of distinction for a game. And it was a game that was recently introduced to America. There wasn't a rulebook, guidebook or instructions. The game of golf needed to be nurtured. The Tufts family seized a vision; it started with James W. Tufts. Ross steered the vision, beginning with horses dragging farming instruments in order to sow the seed that would turn the vision into reality. From a winter resort that offered mild temperatures and relaxation, to one that afforded the golfer a chance to test his ability and will against natural terrain, sculpted and mounded, and varying atmospheric conditions. Pinehurst has weathered its more than 100 years with a perseverance deeply entrenched in the amateur game. And it was James W. Tufts's grandson, Richard S. Tufts, who dedicated his life to pioneering the

Early golf at Pinehurst was about roundish sand greens.

amateur game and holding it to a lofty ideal of sportsman-ship that made the game and the place extremely unique. After all, that was the first game. Bobby Jones, who devel-oped a course in Augusta, Georgia, made another indelible description. He said, "Pinehurst Resort and Country Club is the St. Andrews of United States Golf." Ross knew that the sand of St. Andrews had lent itself to cause acclaim to the Scottish links, just as sand provided the backbone of Pinehurst.

Sure, Ross set up Oakland Hills, Oak Hill, Inverness, Wannamoisett and Seminole. But he made his home just off the third and fifth greens at Pinehurst. And it was Ross, a Scot, who brought a passion of exactness and precision to the sandy soil of Pinehurst. Some call it divine revelation.

His drawings on paper, using topographical maps, changed the game from all angles. And it is the subtleties of his design that are possibly the greatest gifts: the undula-tions in the greens, the sight line off the tees. The little things are the big things at Pinehurst. And Ross might have made his largest contribution in the mid-1930s when up from the sand came the stubble of green grass. *The Pinehurst Out-look* reported, "Until 1935, we did not have sufficient knowl-edge to build and maintain a satisfactory grass putting sur-face for greens in this climate. Consequently, all the greens were what was known then as sand greens…Naturally these sand greens did not have to be mowed, but they had to be maintained." To maintain the green, they used a pile of sand near each green, with old barrels sunk in the ground filled with water. They would add sand and water and then scrape the green with a rake handle attached to a board, which would smooth the surface. The greens were almost perfectly round. But that was the beginning.

Longfellow must have been referring to the No. 2 course, for no course extracts as much physical and mental inertia.

The amateur game was the essence of play at Pinehurst. Richard Tufts was the guardian of the amateur game, and he ushered the game in with integrity, honesty and was the reason the game has an etiquette that transcends generations. Tufts may have been disappointed about some of the doglegs that Pinehurst drove in time, but he ultimately would have been proud of the return to its roots. A shrug of the shoulders and a nod of the head might have been the gesture to acknowledge the return of the U.S. Open to Pinehurst in 2005. But knowing that the 2007 U.S. Amateur is heading to Pinehurst is more fitting. "When you come to Pinehurst there are so many choices to make," Fay said of the Pinehurst Course offerings. "We feel so linked to this special place. It is truly the special place of American golf." And Tufts's greatest contribution to golf may not be associated to Pinehurst, but rather his contribution to the rules of golf. Bill Campbell said, "There is no question that his legacy has to include his role in the movement toward uniformity of the rules of golf. It started in 1951, but did not really end until 32 years later."

Pinehurst wasn't discovered by the USGA or anyone else in 1999. It was re-discovered.

And the progression of the game of golf remains bunkered in values, integrity and honor, things that ring true at Pinehurst like the chimes on the village chapel.

The greens complex at Pinehurst is a combination of bunkers, green, and collar; each having slope and angle characteristics. (Photo provided by the Pinehurst Convention and Visitors Bureau.)